AMERICAN
WESTERN SONG

3039-PEAR

Victor Pearn

AMERICAN
WESTERN SONG

---

poems from 1976 to 2001

For Don Prentice

Victor W. Pearn

3039-PEAR

CONTENTS

SANDMAN
AT THE STARDUST ALTAR

WITH
A TWIST OF LIME

MARINE BASIC

Phase One

WHERE
THE RIVER FLOWS

Dedicated to Jesus,

and my mother who believed in me.

Acknowledgements

Sandman at the Stardust Altar *Colorado Daily*, "Fog at Santa Monica,"; *Lynx Eye*, "Mother of Pearl,"; *The Lucid Stone*, "Petals in the Snow,"; *Practum Survo*, "Patience,"; *Seasons of Change*, "Waves,"; *Sunstone*, "Green Cutthroat Trout"; *South Carolina Review*, "Tutoring Tanya and Jessica". With a Twist of Lime *Ahnkhology*, "A Sculptured Song," "Graffiti Artist," "Jogging in Cuernavaca," "Downtown"; *Boulder Planet*, "I Want Taco Bell," "Sunlight Dove," "An Old Rusty Wheelbarrow"; *Lilies of the Field*, "With Jesus," "Oil Paintings". Marine Basic *Vietnam Generation*, "Running,"; *Practum Servo*, "Peace". Where the River Flows *Alchemist Review*, "the maxillofacial surgeon's dog"; *Archer*, "a covered bridge in winter"; *Aster*, "the 4th of july," "before the strike," "letter to rich"; *Bone & Flesh #13*, "liberty"; *Coloradan 1984*, "one year of grace"; *Crazy Quilt Quarterly*, "malvinas"; *Explorer Magazine*, "dream of chicago," "hallowed wood"; *Ihcut*, "to hint of deep winter"; *Inky Blue*, "november"; *Iliad Press*, "tropical shower"; *Long Islander; Walt's Corner*, "nightsound"; *Manna*, "crimson"; *Marharbour Newsletter*, "rain clouds"; *Matrix IV*, "bamboo art," "in this greenhouse"; *Midland Review*, "solar complexities"; *Negative Capability*, "colorado university"; *Omnific*, "snapshot"; *Orphic Lute*, "cavefish for l.l,"; "the view from my window"; *Parting Gifts*, "hard corn"; *Pegasus*, "diggin up wildcherry wine," "in the fieldhouse"; *Poetalk*, "improvisation on birthmarks & body scars"; *Rantoul Press*, "sleigh ride in illinois"; *Red Dancefloor*, "where the river flows"; *Riverrun 1*, "the hump on his back"; *Riverstone*, "the timbre"; *The Scrivener*, "walking in snow before dawn"; *Sulphur River Literary Review*, "pyromaniac"; *Thirteen*, "sweet trees fragrant trees," "earth," "the lyricist," "under northern light," "hand poems"; *Tight*, "western light," "hand poems"; *The Village Magazine*, "prescription for nuclear attack", *We Speak For Peace*, "nichols park". Thanks to the University of Colorado for permission to print *Where the River Flows*.

Sandman
at the Stardust Altar

Fog at Santa Monica

Fog at Santa Monica

sun a white ball
moonlike the ocean is
in a shroud of mist
sand floor and mist
the sky and ocean gone
under a white out

today the bikepath is crowded
unlike any other day crowded
bicycles skaters joggers
and families or couples
out for a walk

the human heart is infinite
a simple truth

it is good to receive
your letter today
before I read it
I walked in thick white fog

Poem at the New Year

dolphin fins rise curving in air
then the nose and tail dive into water

maybe seventy in that
school swimming south
now in this moment of clarity
there is so much the heart desires

hope in shreds damp and clammy
here the homeless hang
foot long beards and beg for change
pushing possessions in carts

under the brown cloud of despair
in this new year
a baby will be born
dolphins gather to celebrate

I hope they will run someone for office
who will do something

A Grain of Sand

a man asked me
to have any change
even one penny
told me he was hungry
he was going through
garbage cans so he could
find some food

I gave him a pocketful
of change all the change
that I had on me
and a five dollar bill

I told him down on your luck
his face lit up
he thanked me twice
as I walked away he yelled
God Bless You

Where Pelicans Glide

pacific in a shroud of gray
no sun
breakwater whitecaps
flowing strong to shore
seven surfers
in black wetsuits
sealions waiting to catch a wave

I am happy
I love the sound of laughter
and those ten foot waves crashing
and I can walk north
along venice beach sand
where somebody has planted
one cut longstem red rose
in this gray muck

Jade Mountain

sycamore forest
in a canyon
sweet clean air
scent of fallen leaves
forest trail here
a winding dirt road
ascending another jade
mountain four horseback
riders gallop past
the last rider says
happy new year

these trees have
moss on their bark
from here you can
see malibu beach
so much can happen
in a new year

you can go from
footprints in the sand
to a colorado
rocky mountain peak
and where ever you go
you will find love

Mother of Pearl

muscles at shell beach
concert violins wedding girls
it takes a grain of sand
to make a pearl
searching for the essence of man
beings from space
take people for an experiment
in the film *Dark City*
at the end what remains
are people and shell beach
inside the oyster shell
is that beautiful
mother of pearl
like weddings and violins
or the smooth trail of a jet
beside the calm ocean
what happens when you
see mother of pearl
what do you think about
it takes one life
to make a soul
sunlight dappled on the water
bodies rubbed with tanning oil

The Ocean's Edge

it was the most beautiful
sunset I have ever seen
I had *inside the actor's studio* on
because I like that program
I left the house in a hurry
fearing I might be late after all
this was life the real show
a glimpse of lovely sunlight
a great fiery red giant
swollen three times
twice its height over the pacific
the sea was lightblue
with white bubbly waves
that crested golden
when they flipped
a pelican skimmed the surface
a few gulls stood along the shore
  the sun dipped through a deep purple cloud
and became a fiery orange giant
casting orange through purple clouds
as it hit the edge of the ocean
and became brilliant gold
leaving a magic pink
mellow glow on moist sand

After the Rose Parade

a kite flier on the sand
his kite six kites in one
full diamonds with solid
rainbow colors and
six long tails matching

a kite salesman gave up drugs
and alcohol turned his face
to the beautiful rainbow kite
soaring and flying away
into the great wind

gulls arrive like angels
to observe on the shore
how kites fly

I am happy leaving my footprints
I cannot see any smog
homeless gather here
huddling in a clump
to share their wine bottles

for everybody homeless
I would give fifteen hundred
loaves of bread
if I had any wealth
why what could anybody do

some lines last
I have saved the best
to soar like the kite you fly
I stop here after the rose parade
not to just survive
may these words prevail

3039-PEAR

Patience

you too will see
the majestic sundown
sunshine lighting surreal
colors on the broad cloud
orange purple gold fire
this cloud an impressionist painting
a high wind blurring the texture
a beautiful God pleasing sky
you could melt a clock
on this outcropping or that nimbus
or you could see a woman's face
under an exposed brain
with a long tongue on the canvas
but this does not shock you
my mother tried to teach me
the value of patience

Sandman

pumpkin cranberry muffin please
from perry's pizza and more
under an umbrella
at a table on the beach
sunshine on my neck
I sit here and write sandman
with a pen in my notebook
the stars and stripes wave
and the state flag with that
california bear it is
the time of the clinton impeachment
trial but nobody is stunned
I count eight volleyball nets
wonder where all these players came from
you can rent skates and bikes here
north pier has a ferris wheel
and a roller coaster
roars with surf edging a calm sea
here too are gulls pigeons
cormorants pelicans and sandpipers
a few shells not many on shore
here are people from germany
south america and england
palm trees grow tall in stature
fragrant eucalyptus leaves
provide a sweet aroma

Meditation on Running

it was a cooing turtledove
in the morning beside a delightful
waterfall

it was a refreshing run
along santa monica beach

a sunshine ballet on water
a perfect movement

what about pollution
what about homeless souls
the sick poor and hungry

breaking a sweat
I ran breathing salt spray

Poem at the Marina

past crowds of pelicans
and sharp beaked cormorant
the kayaker rows up the marina
a sailboat turns the corner
a breeze carries it to the pacific
the wind full in three sails
rowing with a strong oar
a man with a rhythm
it is something to see
a kayaker beside another sailboat
strives for a workout I guess
he challenges and they race
with eager crews
deepsea fishing boats crawl by
after a big catch of seabass or tuna
followed by crying gulls
hoping to gather scraps
a sloop and coastguard cutter
travel the marina they
exit the santa monica harbor
leaving a whitewater trail

Down a Blacktop Road

Promise of the Future

Zest and gusto
during this flight
on the way to my daughter's wedding
three children
sit in front of me
they color in books.
At Salt Lake city
I change planes.
A crowd with welcome banners
balloons and cameras
look for their missionary youth.
They get off the plane
I will fly to Denver in.
These people are alive.
I am a fortunate witness
when the group shows up
there are cheers, big smiles
and hugs. The crowd lingers.
This flight three more children
are in the row in front of me.
They color red valentines
for their Mother.

Faith in Jesus

Some of my answered prayers:
Charley's daughter Amanda
healed of a heart problem.
My acceptance at Colorado
University Graduate school.
The release of three American
prisoners of war in Kosovo.
When I was twenty-two
in Hawaii, many people
prayed for me as I was
dying from a bad kidney
and through skilled surgery
I was healed completely.
A daughter to stop smoking.
A poem that won an award.
My daughters' high school
graduation. February's wedding.
A safe trip to Mission Mazahua
in Mexico. Prayers work.

Prayers

Family by name for seven generations
into the future,
for peace on earth and in my heart,
for wisdom, understanding, and knowledge
and common sense
to keep our democracy strong,
safe and free
our President, Vice President,
the House, the Senate, the Judicial
branches of government
all of our leaders, our schools,
every man, woman and child
in the American military,
surround them with angels
protect them with your kindness
and love, I pray that no one
would die today.
All American veterans, a blessing on all who
visit the Vietnam war memorial
and on the Vietnamese people
hungry, poor, sick, lost, lonely,
downtrodden people, the homeless
and jobless people with Mental Illness,
Aids, Muscular Dystrophy, Leukemia,
Lupus, Cancer of any type, those with
any handicap, the deaf, the blind
for many who are sick by name
for specific hospitals, medical

centers and dental offices,
blessings for the doctors,
nurses, staff and volunteers
and for awesome, tremendous, miraculous
healing power to work anywhere,
for many Pastors by name and
for Churches, Missionaries, Gideons,
Promise Keepers and Christians,
for God's will in their lives.
Thank you Jesus for many blessings
and for answered prayer.

Poem at the Wedding

Stuffed elk says
that was the best
wedding I ever saw.

The bride lovely
and beautiful
in her majestic
noble gown,
a princess, she
held her bouquet
of pink roses
because it was
on Valentines Day.

The groom sharp
in his bow tie,
a valiant prince,
in his air force
dress uniform
with high glossed
shoes better
for a physics
major to fly with.

It was radiant joy
bright smiles with love
waves of love unconditional.

Stuffed Elk

Why does the stuffed elk speak?
I celebrate life.
Why was the elk head stuffed
and hung up on a wall?
That is a celebration of death.
If you hunt elk,
then your family eats it to live
there is nothing wrong with that.
If you stuff an elk to preserve beauty
and hang him on a wall
there is nothing wrong with that,
but I might call you
a member of the hunting herd
a family of elk.

I Found an Afternoon

I walk in
the mountains.

Green grasses
and deeper green
pines capture
my gaze.

I sit on a rock,
listening to the
meadow lark's
opera tenor,
and bluetail
swallow's twitter.

I would put
my roots down here
like a pine,
lift my branches
to the sky,
sway in wind.

Watch the clouds expand
over mountain ridges.

Or as the immovable rock
I rest on, remain
steadfast here always.
I have another purpose.

With care I descend
the mountain trail
picking flowers.

I nibble
a yellow flower.

Eat three peppergrass
flowers, and
a white petal cluster
with black and gold
bumble bees humming
as they gather
sweet nectar.

I touch Russian olive,
Chinese elm, and
heart shaped,
cottonwood leaves.

I want to
remember their shapes,
their texture,
their color
and fragrance.
I know, in an afternoon,
so much is lost.

Down a Blacktop Road

for Donna June

If I could write
a country song
I'd give it to
Willie Nelson.

Down a blacktop road
my sister walked alone,
because he was
drinkin' and carousin'.
She left home.

When she'd had enough
she hit the road,
went on her own
down that blacktop road.

If I could write
a country song,
the wind's kicking up
I'd give it to Willie Nelson,
and he'd make a million.

A Lion and the Lamb

I have a daughter
named after a rock,
Crystal.

Cynthia, after the
Greek godess
of the moon,

and a daughter
named Spirit.

February, my
youngest daughter
named after
the month.

This year a warm
mild month
it was her month.

I was born in March.
They say March comes in
like a lion,

and goes out
like a lamb,
or sometimes March
comes in like a lamb
and goes out like a lion.

It depends on how the winds blow.

A Lion and the Lamb II

February is also
my Mother's namesake.

Mother was named Dephim.
Those six letters
being the first initials of
her six aunts, so my baby
February Dephim

carries my Mother's name.

With four grown daughter's
ranging in age from twenty-nine
to twenty-one

my hope is to live like a lion
to go out
like a lamb
      hear me roar.

Glacier Gorge

Four Thin Does

gracefully leap the fence
following in line they pause

all at once lift their ears
look back over their shoulders

at the mountains early in spring
and silently in slow motion move on

Bluebird Meadow

like the sky
had fallen
deep blue in
wind a flock
scattered high
across a colorado
meadow beautiful
bluebirds perch
on dry weeds
and weathered
wooden fenceposts
to sing lovely
angelic songs
and begin to fly

Two Grazing Bucks

a four point buck
and a six point buck
stood sublime
chewing grass
their long necks reaching
low for the early spring blades
on my casual approach
the younger buck looked up
his brown eyes the size of quarters
then gently tapped the antlers
of the other buck
until he looked up too
playfully they
clacked antlers a while
the four point buck
walked away north
the six point buck
ate more grass then turned
his head toward me around
to lick his right hind knee joint
and he raised his head up high
stuck out his long tongue
yawned and walked north

A Cloud Like This

I have seen
something I did
not know today.

When I walked
up the mountain
path to the north,

there was rain
in front and behind
me about a mile away.

On the mountain
crest high overhead
two eagles are hanging

in midair stationary.
Floating with windspeed
holding them in place.

I watch them
hold their position
for a long time,

I watch the crack
in the clouds
above them

the blue, and the light
on the cloud edges
and I want to see

Jesus coming on
a cloud like this.
As I meditate

on how great God is
I know I see only
the smallest glimpse.

Rabbit Crossing

emmett brown
the great and noble rabbit
I say that to him
nearly every day
he is the gentlest
best natured creature
I have ever known
I have taken him to the beach
and he leaped right
into the salty waves
he jumped up in the air
and gave a little kick
when the wave came in
shallow on his back feet
then he hopped to the beach
where curious seagulls circled
he has big brown eyes
a little pink nose
brown cheeks around the eyes and ears
brown fur on his back
and back legs
white fur from his nose
to a point between his ears
and on his mouth, chest
front legs and cotton tail
he has no fear
of cats three times his weight
I have no reason

to put a rabbit
in this book of poems
except to make him immortal

And Springtime in Boulder

slow bloom of the willow leaf
and yellow daffodils
I always loved
that row of pink peony

five buck deer
in our yard
eat fresh lilac leaves
in a drizzling mist

Mary Magdalene

wet street
neon signs
electric street car

in a movie scene
an illusion of time
and distance

but in reality
mary magdalene
was the first person

jesus appeared to
when he arose
from death

it was you mary
who was healed
it was you mary

who was first to see
jesus in all his glory
mary it was you

Glacier Gorge

The river was
white like spray
from a fire hose
forced between
solid rock.

Snow covered peaks
were above enchanted
meadows where an elk herd
grazed lazily.
I walked up beside the waterfall

in early june,
in old snow,
drawn by the river's voice.
A giant shower tumbled
through midair in an arc.

And I crossed a wooden bridge,
paused for lunch and shot
a photo of a marshmallow cloud.
Silence in the rock and pine trees
a deep solitude,

and I heard a human voice.
A young woman from Texas.
She came down to me
with her parents, and said
the view was worth

the climb, I was almost there.
The trail went up across two
narrow wooden bridges,
the lake was partially
iced.

A spectacular natural beauty
this forest was
like a dream landscape,
a climb into ice
into fiery cold stardust.

Digging up
a Chinese Elm Stump

I have to dig
around this old elm,
or I will not be able
to write a poem.

It is now apple blossom time
and rain has awakened me.

After I dug a week
and had a mound of dirt
it snowed a foot deep.

When I dug the second
pile of dirt it began to rain
and rain fell all night then snow.

This stump is six feet wide
with a flagstone rock garden
on the west and a link fence
through the center it grew around.

I thought this stump
was my Moby Dick,
and it seemed an impossible task
to dig it up.

Kindness, Justice and Mercy

What if language was not
important after all?

What if you
lived in a city
where everybody
bought one-hundred books of
poetry a year?

What if language has
beauty, truth and power?

Poetry has power
to communicate
kindness, justice and mercy
to the future
to heal a generation,
as yet, unborn.

Petals in the Snow

3039-PEAR

Petals in the Snow

for Columbine High School

Angry gray clouds
rain on top of snow
out my window a flicker woodpecker taps.
When the rain ends
I walk to the market
for fresh rabbit food.
Robins have dark feathers; the distant
mountain range has white hills with
dark clouds rolling across them.
Mansions are folded neat
into the hills jagged stone outcroppings,
long needle pines stand tall.
In snow covered meadows
where I hear new music—
cheerful birds chirping.
On my way home I notice
nature everywhere in black,
white, or a gray scene.
A dark sky over the brilliant earth.
I am surprised to find
yellow Columbine blossoms and pink
apple petals in the snow.

A Rustle of Wind

Do you hear
the leaves rustle
on a windy day?
Have you heard
the male and female
bluebirds sing?
Have you heard the river
flow down a mountain?
Have you breathed
pine fragrance?
Have you seen the shimmer
of golden aspen leaves
on a clear October day?
Do you try to see
what is at work
in every circumstance
in everyday life?
Have you held
a puppy, a kitten,
or a bunny rabbit?
Have you sailed
on the high sea,
ran a marathon,
or snow skied
down copper mountain?

Night Crawler

On this sad day
I am troubled
by a dead squirrel.
I fix my gaze
on the abyss
and say a prayer,
troubled I cannot
bring the squirrel back.
That is not within my power.
I catch a night crawler
it feels cold in my hand,
and wiggles to escape.
I take it
to some dry leaves
tangled below a bush,
a Japanese quince.
I am thinking of my daughters
now raising their own families
and the distance between us.
Although, the old dirty snow melts
it lingers with endurance.

House Sitting

While my friend
David, and Jeanne his wife
who is a Blackfoot
Indian and a lawyer,
and their lovely
teenaged daughter Abi
are in Italy, I
am taking care
of their house,
cars, and dog Lucy.
Twice this house
has been in
"Better Homes
and Gardens" magazine.
I water the plants
inside and outside.
I take the trash
and recyling out.
Every day I feed
the dog twice
bring in the papers,
and the mail.
This house is spacious
filled with light.
Columns in the dining
room were topped with white crosses.

I mow the lawn, prune the trees,
and walk the dog.
I do not like sleeping here.
I prefer sleeping in my own bed.

3039-PEAR

This Night's Dilemma

I cannot sleep
I cannot work
I cannot write.

I cannot write
and earn a living
I cannot work
and write.

What am I to do,
rain hammering shingles?

Jacksonville Poets

Reg had blond hair
when I met him.
He loved to read
Donald Duck comic books,

eat penny candy.
We both read books at
the Carnegie endowed
public library.

We grew up in
the same home town.
A place where
young men dreamed

of athletic careers
to find a way out.
We both went to
Illinois University.

Now he has snow-white
hair. Although we
are both Jacksonville
poets, our lives seem

parallel. He left town
before I was born.
We met in Boulder
at Colorado University.

Reg Saner attended my first
poetry reading there.
He became my thesis
advisor and mentor.

Letter to John Knoepfle

John, your few words are vast
as the pacific
with its mountain ranges,
wide mouthed rivers
feeding it fresh water
from the highest mountaintops.
From intricate islands,
moonlight shimmers with
shore-to-shore liberty: for surfers,
jellyfish, sharks, flying fish,
whales, dolphins,
starfish, seahorses, clams,
crabs, coral, urchins.
Salmon swim upstream jumping
into the jaws of grizzlies.
Sunlight a dapple
on the water and salt spray.
Every night a new sailboat
casts a golden sail into the sun's eye,
like your fierce poetry,
seeking the shortest
passage to the heart.
Every night couples walk
on the pier, ride the ferris wheel
and go barefoot in the sand.
Holding hands lovers kiss
like waves lapping the beach.

Sharpened Number Two Pencils

Richard Hugo and I
walked together
under mature elms
that whispered to us
this must be a great
place to spend the
rest of your life.
At "The Sink" restaurant
on the hill in Boulder
we ate banana splits
and talked about poetry.
I got to know him
for two weeks at
the writer's conference.
He impressed me
when he recited his
poetry from memory
for an hour to an
audience of two-hundred.
Richard, Bill Matthews,
and I, won a game of
basketball on the asphalt
at University Hill school.
He used to say, "All you need
to write is a handful
of sharpened number two pencils,
and a yellow tablet."
He sent me a letter from

Missoula saying things were grim.
He was solid like a mountain.
He used to drive to ghost towns,
and reservoirs to find a poem.
In WWII he went through
German cities that were rubble
from concentrated bombing.
When he died I read an article
in the paper by a man who
once took him to watch Dr. J.
play pro basketball, and the
joke was on him because
he imagined the Dr. would
be Jewish, and wanted to
see how he played.

The Salute

A parade came by
bringing his
horse drawn casket.

A boy gave
a smart salute.

The sound of
horses hooves.
The sound of drums.

A Bold Chipmunk

Under a giant cloud
he peeks his head out
on pink granite
to see what
all the commotion
is on the trail,
then climbs on a fallen
aspen for a better look.
He finds a pear core
on a rock, sniffs
the scent of a large
creature who left it,
and holds the sweet pear
in his paws
eating seeds and all.
There are two goldfish
cheddar crackers on the rock.
After eating
the pear, he pushes the
goldfish into his cheeks
and scurries home for a snack.

Green Cutthroat Trout

Mind Eraser

Courage a blue rose
inside gathers like
a lump in the throat.
At the amusement park
where no self-respecting
poet would go on
the mind eraser.

A red metal chair
you are strapped into
hung from a monorail
propelled by a chain.
It rises and dips,
twists like a roller coaster
screws around four times
legs flying free,
then flips you twice
with such force that
your body remains seated,
while your mind erases.

It was Father's day,
waiting our turn
the hour a lightning bolt
dispersed the crowd.
We were first when
the ride resumed.
Kipp my son-in-law,

and my daughter in
the first two chairs.
I was in the third
behind my daughter.
She was happy to see me.

A thrill and a challenge.
The heart quiet
the mind clear,
nothing like
running a Marine
obstacle course.

Boulder

Again reading Walt,
like an American catalog.

A busker
on Pearl Street
folds himself
into a box
says someday
he'll be on
Letterman.

Fireworks over
the Colorado football stadium.

Breakfast at Chautauqua,
literature, music and art.

Deer, bear, rabbits,
raccoons, rattle snakes,
great blue herons,
eagles, falcons, hawks,
owls, wild turkey,
black squirrels—
a few natives.

Don't forget the buffalo,
green light at sunrise,

world class runners,
bikers, kayakers, mountain climbers
motorcyclers, ice skaters,
skiers, dancers, gymnasts,
and the summer
Shakespeare Festival.

Stores and shoppers,
window panes and
wildflowers with
vacationing yellow
butterflies,

what is Boulder,
A collection of stone;
a pile of rock.

A Sprinkle of Stardust

Buttermint, the last hoop
that you go through,
at the pearly gate.

Jesus, at the altar,
for those who built
their lives on the rock.

Welcome home,
obedient and faithful . . .
child, welcome home.

For those who built
on the sand, when
the storm came, they

were washed away.
They didn't make it
to the last hoop.

A blinding rainbow
behind his altar, the river
of life flowing out.

Jesus, give us peace,
sprinkle us with stardust,
make us shine like the stars.

Green Cutthroat Trout

speckled and hidden by rocks
in water from glaciers compressed 1500 years
trout thrive

open mouthed they float to the surface
their tails and fins wave
as slowly as angel wings

when they leap they fly into a new world
the aspen trees and starlight
and we watch them marveling as their gills burn
breathing fresh air

then they swerve and fall
deep on their way home
like an emerald in colorado water

Working Two Jobs For Rent

I flew like Superman once
when my bike hit a curb
and threw me like a wild bronco.

I landed on concrete
favoring my left side,
maybe protecting my only right kidney.

Scraped my hand, elbow, hip, ankle,
foot, bruised two upper ribs, and
cracked my kneecap, all on the left.

Doctor told me bones are always being
replaced. They are always in their teens.
Even at 95 your bones are early twenty.

Flat on my back with my knee up packed
in ice for a week, I thought, sometimes
life is so hard, you cannot get a cool

glass of water. By yourself
striving is useless, empty as
words can be empty, without love.

Buckskin and Palomino

the buckskin had
a black mane and tail
the palomino had
a blond mane and tail
the buckskin was the
alpha male of the herd
they were both quarterhorses
the fastest horse in the quarter
mile good for cattle
the palomino was small
a female the buckskin stallion
had wild horse marking
dark around the ear tips
with a dark stripe
on his back between his hips
he was gentle
a good temperament
I met them walking eagle trail
I was going up the steep
incline toward the mesa
and they were coming down
when I got to the mesa top
there was a panoramic view
after a while I went down
and met the horses again
on the side of the trail
munching purple prairie clover
they both had saddles

and riders there was a rancher
a male on the stallion and
the ranch owner a woman on the
palomino we walked in the
same direction for a mile
the buckskin came over
and said hello the woman
said she lost her shirt I told
them I had seen it about two thirds
of the way up the trail to the mesa
the man on the buckskin said he would
go back and get the shirt and meet her
at the ranch she pointed out the horses
that were hers on the otherside of the fence
eagle trail went past a pond
and got narrower I walked ahead
the palomino mare really liked me
and kept nuzzling against my shoulder
I petted her jaw face neck ears
brushed a fly from her stomach
animals like me people do not
it made the woman on the mare laugh
after we reached the otherside
of the pond she ran the palomino
all the way up the hill as fast as she could go
for a workout the mare waited
at the top of the hill for the stallion
where I had just walked
I watched the stallion
galloping down across the trail
raising a dust cloud

Elk Antlers

Elk fight
to establish a
dominant male in
autumn before mating.
The most aggressive fighter
is not always the largest.
A man on a buckskin horse
says, "its not the size
of the dog in the fight;
it's the size of the
fight in the dog."
I tell him that was
a bit of wisdom
my brother used to
tell me. The elk
who wins has to mate
with every female
in the herd. That burns
up his winter fat,
and he can't survive
a harsh winter. But,
sometimes they do survive.
You should see his huge rack of antlers.

Prayer Warrior

I run in wildflower meadows
   where buffalo ran.
I pray, sometimes when
   I am running.
People who run don't know
   I am praying.
People who pray don't know
   I pray running.

One new prayer
is like a feather
on a hill crest
above wonderland lake meadow.
Spreading my arms out
I imagine feathers
around my head, neck, down my back,
along my arms.

I pray on my knees.

Like eagle wings.
Like an eagle gliding the thundercloud.

Red Stardust

In just a second
your cell phone will ring
and an attorney
will say he is returning
your manuscript from your literary agent's
estate because she is deceased.

Then, there will be a knock
on your door and the mail carrier
will give you a bag of letters
from magazine editors
with advance checks.
The letters will offer
a free lifetime subscription,
ask you to submit your poetry.

And you will bathe in money
like Scrooge McDuck. Having a poet's mind
is to let the vixen fox
tell your story,
or a python who has
not eaten for a year.
Same as owning a
metaphor café in simile county.

Light travels away from stars.
A red stardust cloud
illuminates a nebulous galaxy
gravity collapses the cloud,
in just a second, to create
a new star.

Tutoring Tanya and Jessica

Monet's Bridge

Our galaxy
a potter's wheel, pinwheel
shooting and starlight

flowers open
floating on a pond
emerald light

flowing from the canvas
blotches of paint caked,
it might be a willow tree

what water there is
reflecting shades of green
no sky except a sky blue

bridge thrown over the pond
a bridge where I would
like to walk

let this bridge be the end
where you look
at everything in movement

through everlasting time
I would stand there
under the light of Pegasus.

Fields Ripe for Harvest

Orange moon
throws its back out
above fields ripe for harvest.

My mother,
born in the Texas
pan-handle during dustbowl

moved at the tender
age of seven with her mom and dad,
and two sisters to the level plains of Illinois.

Where fields had
muscle, and fertile black
earth was surrounded with flowing rivers.

In a one room
school with dad from
kindergarten mom graduated with honors.

He helped
spring planting fall
harvest, dropping out after eighth grade.

A farm hand
he did custom work
using his tractor to plow and cultivate.

Before World War
Two, leaving mom and my three
sisters and brother for the National Guard.

Farmers could
afford their own equipment
by the end of the war, his job was gone.

He drove cattle
and hogs to the slaughter house,
then when mom was pregnant with me he left.

Mom moved into
a small city and took
a waitress job when a quarter was

considered a big tip.
I was the fifth child and we
lived in a one room apartment battling poverty.

I was raised
by my mother before
being a single parent was acceptable.

Dad died
when I was sixteen
he had had a difficult life.

I had only
two memories of Forrest
and stories of those who knew him.

I was the baby
in my family, fatherless
in a place of disadvantage and chaos.

Mother taught
Sunday School at the
Centenary Methodist Church. Her Bible

was a Greek New Testament.
I joined the Marines during Vietnam
both for discipline and for honor and glory.

I'm the first
university graduate
from my hard working family.

I never heard
voices of my grandparents
who died long before I was born in Illinois.

I carry them
now inside my heart into
the new century beyond the year 2001.

Rain Dance

As it was for the Anasazi.
As it swelled mountain streams
that fed meandering
muddy rivers flowing to the gulf.
As it made corn swell
into a thick green sea.
As pure drops hung
on golden wheat.
As it refilled shrunken
buffalo wallows from drought
quenching flaming skulls.
As it showered wild-eyed
brown rabbit fur.
As it washed away red dirt
from Colorado buffalo.
As it plopped gently
on summer jade leaves;
as on the snow-white feathers
of wild swans in cattails.
As it summoned thunderheads
to in-fold fire for a rainbow.

Rickshaw Laundry

cranes etched in glass
opening a fortune
cookie of an eight year old girl
its her first job
in her parent's laundry

now along the great wall
a chorus of voices
lift their song in jubilee toward heaven
you do great things you succeed
you spread your wings and fly

like morning sunlight

Canadian Geese

Sugar maple leaves are fringed in crimson
and Canadian geese fly in a V.
They tell me geese take turns leading;
eerie sounds come from the back
encouraging leaders to persist.
I went out at midnight once
to study the stars at Kaneohe Bay.
I was amazed when a flock of geese appeared.
Now years later, another V with brilliant breasts
make that unforgettable, hysterical honking cry,
wavering into a golden dazzle of aspen trees.

Pearl Moon

Now in morning's
first peach-light
roses bloom and sing
like a choir

and the burning mouth of the wind
hugs every child
kisses every leaf
makes the grass
wave like an ocean.

Now the pearl emerges,
a perfect sphere
pink and rosy cheeked.

Dream in Madrid

At Madrid
dinner in courses
bread and wine
soup, salad, fish and potatoes,
flan and a new friend.
Up until now
my college group
had seen Toledo,
Segovia and Avila,
the Prado, bullfights,
castles, Cathedrals and
a jousting tournament.
Two lovely American coeds
joining my friend
and me for dinner
were in need of escorts.
They lived in Santa Monica.
I was a junior at Illinois.
We walked arm in arm
window shopping and returned
to Hotel Metropol.
After midnight
iron bars locked us out.
A street sweeper came by and waved.
Beside the river
past patios and flower gardens, we
walked holding hands.
In grass, that night we kissed,

water sprinklers came on.
We looked at a statue of Cervantes
went for donuts and cocoa.
They boarded an autobus for Paris.
Would we meet again?
I spent a few days more
at the Hemingway hangouts
with a dream of writing poetry.

Waves

Walking to the beach

at sunset
light has compassion
on dancing whitecaps

they leap like deer
caressing golden light
illumines abstract

tips of waves
thrown into mist
at Santa Monica

I would breathe ocean air
I had to see
each sunset bloom

watch clouds as colorful
as the painted desert—
lone silhouette

like a sailboat, passing through
the sun, as it dips its toe
under the horizon,

a surfer carries his board.

The Frank Shorter Mural

Frank Shorter's legs
are like whitewater
rushing down a mountainside.
Before he won his
gold medal in the marathon
a race bandit jumped
into the finish and ran into
the stadium ahead of him.
Fooling the audience, they
applauded the first runner
and were unusually quiet
when Frank crossed the finish line.
Four years later he actually did
come in second and received the
silver medal. He missed the winners
reward of crowd applause
for achieving his goal.
Twenty-five years later
he received the roar of crowd cheer
when he was honored in the Bolder Boulder
10K race on Memorial day.
The Friday before
a mural named after him was unveiled
on the northeast corner of Spruce and Broadway.
I had been invited by the painter,
Jim Nelson and sat beside him
in the front row. Frank Shorter
stood at the podium and gave a brief talk,

then unveiled the Frank Shorter mural.
In the mural Frank is fourteen feet tall
and leading a race. Behind him the lead pack
life size runners, my friend David Whiteing
is there, then runners trail off like
a meandering river in the distance.
In the background the flatiron mountains.
After the unveiling it was like
an ice cream social, everybody who came
sat around on plastic chairs eating
ice cream with a flat wooden spoon.
Most of the people in the mural
were here with their families.
Exhilaration was in the air.
Frank came over and introduced himself,
asked me to run beside him in the race
with five or six other runners
who would come into the stadium
with him in a group.
I was so thrilled and honored
to be asked to share his moment
of glory.
The group would run at
a slow pace, two minutes slower
than his actual race pace for his
silver and gold Olympic medals,
at around four and a half minutes
per mile but the pace of six
and a half minutes was faster
than I could run a 10K. My fastest
mile was clocked indoors at 5:56,
ten years before and with only
three days before the race I didn't
have time to get in shape.
I graciously declined his offer.

When Frank was a young man
running against boys his age
he could always run farther and faster
than any of those boys
without feeling short of breath.
His barrel chest, which, gave him
superior lung capacity, lean body,
and long legs, enhanced his natural talent
and gave him a high performance level
to begin his training.
He ran up the razorback foothills into
the mountains, ran wind sprints at the track,
and ran on those
well manicured blades of grass
on the campus of Colorado University.
The mural brought together—
painter, poet, world class athlete.

Tutoring Tanya and Jessica

These are two affable intelligent chicana students
in their first year at the university.
They are hungry for knowledge.
They want to know what words
like *procurement* and *innovative* mean.
        I am tutoring them in political science.

    We meet once a week
in the dorm complex commons at Williams Village.
We relax on a loveseat and easy chairs
      around a large round end table.
It is the kind of furniture you might
expect to find in any American home.

Jessica sits on my left. Jessica is summer.
      Tanya sits on my right. Tanya is winter.
      It is a balmy spring evening.
      Jessica is wearing a hot cinnamon
        candy red sweatshirt turned inside out
            with matching red lipstick and nail polish.

She is wearing blue jean cutoffs and slouches back
with her feet on the table, her red socks and long legs.
Tanya is dressed in aquamarine mountain mint socks
          matching plaid and white shorts and solid tee shirt.
Her feet are up in the chair, her knees up, her legs apart.
She gently rubs the skin under the left thigh

with her finger tips and pink nails,
          then she plays with her beautiful brown hair.
          We have a lively discussion on how to
          re-invent government how to save money
          by one stop shopping like putting voter registration
                    in the same place we go for a driver's license.

We discuss re-inventing financial aid for students.
We laugh a lot. They both have beautiful brown eyes
that glisten when they smile, and long brown hair.
          Best friends since the fifth grade, although taking poly sci
was accidental, they tell me they do everything together.
I am a timberwolf lost in the wilderness.

With
a Twist of Lime

for Kayley

Crossing the Bridge

Golden sunlight
rolled on the folds
of the giant Mexican flag
as it rippled in the wind
at dawn on the bridge
crossing the Rio Grande
at Laredo Texas.

The van was packed
with fifteen wheelchairs,
walkers and crutches for
native people near Mexico City.
The Mexican border patrol inspected
the van and sent us back to Laredo.
We needed our missionary letter
to be officially stamped by
Immigration before we could
enter the country.

The American border patrol
said try bridge number two.
At bridge two they sent us back,
told Rich to keep in the right lane
when he crossed bridge one.

On our fifth try crossing the river,
(we had to pay each time)
we went right, into a loading dock
where all the truckers were inspected.

Loading Dock

This is not a story
about cannibalism for survival,
its about social
and cultural change.
Now where were we,
oh yes, Rich had
just parked the van
at the loading dock.
We were close to the
giant green, white and red
Mexican flag, and beside the river.
We gave our papers to a young woman.
After twenty minutes she returned
she wanted us to follow her,
she waved the big rigs
to the left and right
clearing a path for us.
We backed into the dock,
a cement wall seven feet high.
She motioned for me to come
with her, she led me
to the end of the dock,
up the stairway on the dock,
then back to the van
up two outside metal stairways
to a large office with many desks.
She spoke to me in Spanish,
told me to wait and someone

would help me stamp my papers.
I sat there two hours.
Rich sat in the van
using the time to write a speech
in Spanish he would deliver
before giving away wheelchairs
at the mission.

Immigration

The office was like
sitting in a bureaucratic
building in Denver.
I did not speak their language
very well and people
ignored me while
following their normal
work routines. I got up
and asked for someone
who could speak English. I
was told, when the Director
arrived he would stamp my
letter and send me to a place
for a temporary permit
for the van. It would
be close to thirty more minutes.
I went downstairs
to explain the delay
to Rich, then went back
and sat down to wait.

The Director came
then a young woman asked me
to come into his office. I was
underdressed wearing raggedy
bluejean cutoffs and a CU Buffalo
t-shirt. He got right to the point
asking, "Who sent you?"
Another young woman

was interpreting
I explained in our letter
Mission Mazahua
requested wheelchairs.

The Director said we had to
drive back to Laredo unload
he'd give us a permit
to go seven blocks
for another permit.
I said, "We are here now.
My friend is downstairs
he's paraplegic cannot
climb upstairs. We will not
go back to Laredo again, or
unload, that would take
too much time. Its Wednesday
we must be at the mission
by Saturday. The Director
then sent for a man
who spoke excellent English.
He explained the problem
in the letter was the words
medical equipment.
I assured him we didn't have
anything like that. I asked
him to come downstairs to see.
He said we'd have to go back
to Laredo. I said, "that is not
possible." Then he said he
might be able to help,
he came down and looked
inside the van, and asked
if we'd agree to pay a tax.
And we agreed to pay.

He went away and returned
ten minutes later saying
it would be $85. American
money. He got into his new
GMC pickup and paraded us
up a one way street the wrong way
through a truck inspecting gate
right back to where we were the
first time we crossed the bridge.

He went inside a door.
Two men in white shirts
came out. Conveniently
they had a bank inside.
We paid our tax, and
went to another place
for Immigration papers.
Rich gave me ten dollars
to tip the man, but he
warned us to avoid giving
money to anybody.
Two boys waiting beside
our van's wheelchair lift
tried to sell us Mexican
candy for a quarter.

Paper Work

We were told
to go seven blocks,
and the place
was on the left.
When we got there
we were looking
to the right distracted
by the beautiful
water fountain,
the Plaza De Dolphins.
We drove two miles
out of our way
through downtown
traffic, in New Laredo,
before we realized
we had passed it.
I went in to purchase
the little sticker
for our windshield.
This place was like
registering for college.
Go to one place
for the proper form,
fill it out, and take
the form to another
station, then get
a new form, go
to the station where

you will need nine
copies of everything:
passport, drivers license,
immigration permit,
birth certificate, insurance,
and the forms they required.
If you need insurance
you can buy it there.
Then pay ninety dollars
for the windshield sticker;
a temporary auto permit
to drive a vehicle in
Mexico. Don't forget
to return that sticker
when you leave the
country, or you will
be fined eight-hundred
dollars, and since they
have your credit card,
it will be an automatic
charge because you
signed it when they
gave you the auto
permit. And I went
through the process,
paid, and was told to
take a seat and wait.
I was the only person
in the room with blond
hair, and blue eyes.
After twenty or more
minutes about a dozen
names were called out.
Mine was one of them.
We were told to go

get into our cars and
line them up, and somebody
would come around with
our auto permit sticker,
and put it in the upper
driver's side, on the inside
glass. I went out and told
Rich to get in line for the
sticker, and went over
to a public bathroom.
A woman there charged
me two pesos, then she
offered me three sheets
of toilet paper.

Desert into Mountains

The first three hours driving
into Mexico the landscape
was like Texas brush
that became desert
out miles in front mountains
were folds of wrinkled
earth that climbed up
in peaks.
I drove over the summit;
people crowded the tollway.
Two hours before sunset
I approached Monterey,
then turned right traveling
due west towards Saltillo
and more peaks loomed
north and south
in a valley flooded
with golden light
in the wind's eye
as the sun dipped
slowly below the level desert.
A powder blue haze
came on the horizon.
An hour before dark
the road began to curve
in foothills and there
was a crowd of big rigs
speeding to weave

in and around,
then city lights winked
from Saltillo
where I stopped
my first night
at the inn.

Superbowl XXXII

At the inn I clicked on the TV
Bronco players were running
onto the field in San Diego,
so it was on wednesday night
I watched Superbowl XXXII
between the cheeseheads
and Broncos. I have not been
a Packer fan since Bart Starr
played quarterback, in my teens.
Elway and Davis were Denver's
star players, and Atwater at free
safety played the best game
of his career. So far then
at half time I went to eat
at the inn's restaurant.
They catered to Americans
because most of their
executive guests worked
for the nearby Chrysler plant.
I was able to eat
a fine meal and watch
the Broncos' first Superbowl
victory in Spanish.

The Little City Lights

The little cities
have a central plaza
where bouquets of red roses
are sold in the street
by pretty women,
if you are looking.
Walk up the avenue
there are red pots
in shop windows, and red
chili peppers are strung.
There's a delicious aroma
of fresh baked goods.
VW taxis park in line.
Waiting for a fare
in a Dallas Cowboy jersey,
a young driver knows English.
Says when he saves
money he is going
back to Kansas City.
You might see that
solid lime green hotel,
an old man in boots
and a stetson hat
will shake your hand
in sunshine, and offer
a room for the night.
There will be a bank
and a money exchange.

A tiny Catholic church.
The streets will be busy
traffic will be heavy,
and you might think
as I did, this must be
a perfect place.

I want taco bell

stopping for tacos
at an outdoor barbecue
steak and chicken
roasting on a wood
fire the mouth watering
aroma permeated
the street and several
trucks were parked
there men were
laughing while they
ate standing around
the counter and two
women cooked
for ten pesos I
had a chicken taco
smothered with
grilled onions and
green chili sauce
with a coke it tasted
so good and one
man talked with me
in english he said
he was saving money
to go back to iowa
and become a chef
the next day was I
sick I thought I had
spinal meningitis it was
montezumas revenge

Guardian Angel

Traveling I have
seen the cattle on
a thousand hills, fat
or skinny. I haven't
seen my guardian angel.
Perhaps a host of angels
travel down the road with
me, but I don't know much
about angels. Except
in the Bible they usually
say, "Be not afraid,
I bring you good news."
And that is what I like.

Sunlight Dove

A ray of light
broke through the roof
on the west wall
in the shape of a bird.

A luminous image of
the universal Holy Spirit,
in flight on the white adobe
at Mission Mazahua

unnoticed by anyone.
As disabled children
teenagers and a
woman with no legs
received their first wheelchair,
the sunlight dove

floated clockwise.
As joy overcame
families in Mexico who
had carried relatives here,
or pushed them
in a wheelbarrow.

Wheelchair Caravan

There is dignity
in the gift received.
Families have joyful
tears on red cheeks.
For children and teens
men and women,
it is the first time
they will know mobility.
They wheel in line
for a group photograph,
everybody says cheese.
Then they caravan into
a Mission banquet feast
to eat potato, carrot, zucchini,
chicken soup, with steamy
bluecorn tortillas, beans, rice,
with a twist of lime,
avocados stuffed with fish,
lemonade, coffee and cake,
and they give thanks
for all those blessings.

Bells and Fireworks

Bombs explode at five a.m.
announcing before dawn
the Festival de Candelaria.
Cathedral bells are rung
by hand. The rope pulled
up and down, up and down,
everyday until the Festival,
fireworks go for ten minutes,
then bells for ten minutes,
for an hour and a half.
This creates a rhythm
in concert with fireworks
shocking as cannon fire,
booming like a large drum
exploding into song.

Wall of Flames

Fire, vultures, and dead dogs,
were what I saw most
on the drive into Mexico.
Wearing purple shorts,
white shoes, and a singlet, I jog
along the cobblestone street.
A blazing sun, and a cold wind
twist up dust devils
three hundred feet high
as I go out the mission gate.
The narrow path trails east
around the crumbling Cathedral.
I run downhill on the left.
A police car nearly
runs me over, and I go
right, slip on loose gravel
and fall. Fortunately I am
not injured. A fire blazes
five feet high. Smoke rises
darkly into the clear sky,
and it is difficult to breathe.
Along the road here, farmers
regularly burn off
dead brown foliage
wasting fine organic mulch.
A wall of flame dances up.

With Jesus

walk the cobblestone streets
inside the mission look
at the red, yellow
blue and green color
of the stained glass
windows with stars
snowflakes and butterflies
crosses to remind you
what peace you can have
come into the dining hall
where the scent of food
is heavenly and the two
long long tables are surrounded
with hand carved wooden chairs
that make you think you might
be dining in a medieval castle
where ivy grows fresh
on the eaves all year
the roof has red dirt tile
one bell one small cross
a blue eyed siamese cat and
a chocolate short hair dog
with golden eyes live here too

Hacienda

Stones laid there
in 1718 when the church
was built and the perfectly
curved bells set in the steeple.
The hacienda that became
Mission Mazahua was added
with wall, gate and fence.
Goats graze inside keeping
lawns manicured, and are
returned to their corral.
Pink eyed rabbits are scratching
and bathing and sitting up
cocking their ears to listen
from their cages nearby.
In the cathedral oil paintings
Mary, Joseph, Jesus and more
originals, gorgeously preserved.
In the mission a soccer field,
a mansion for many guests,
iris, lilies, and many colorful
flowers are blossoming along the wall.
Singing sparrows are a surprise,
and the distant soft cooing turtledove.
Standing in noble contrast
a giant tree without leaves, or bark, dead
outside the western mission wall.

An Old Rusty Wheelbarrow

A teenage boy arrives
at the mission in a wheelbarrow.
His mom has a sad look
as his dad lifts him up.
No Humpty Dumpty fairy tale
he has dignity and patience
his toddler sister plays in sunlight
always near him she never goes far.
They sit on the garden wall
beside the wheelbarrow,
and a yellow blanket
he uses for a cushion.
He doesn't know he is going to receive
a new wheelchair.
His mom and dad
go greet the other families
as they gather, and share
a moment of friendship, and laughter.
I sit by the immobile teen
try to photograph another boy
who is shy and runs
behind his mother, or
pulls his shirt over his face,
or dodges behind his
colorful serape.

The paraplegic boy beside me laughs
each time I raise my camera
and the shy boy hides.
His peaceful face is bright
when he smiles with laughter.
He is calm and cheerful.
Today for his surprise
he is one of seven people who
receive their first wheelchairs.
I go to my apartment for a new chair,
and wheel his out to him.
His dad helps him into the chair;
it's a stunning miracle
to see the joyful faces,
parents and their children too.
Now they wheel around by grace
and their own strength.
The face of the laughing boy
is the same as God's face.
When those people wheel
themselves into the dining room
they give thanks to God,
and break their bread together.
The toddler eats beside her brother.
When the meal is over, and
the families have gone,
I walk through the courtyard.

It is empty, beautiful
as it was before,
and I can't help but notice
the old rusty wheelbarrow
with a yellow blanket in tatters
that is left behind.

Ascent

Someday the children
from this mission will
rise up and do great
things. They will swim
and lift weights. They
will play games and run.
They will go skiing down
the powdery slopes
in Colorado because
the gospel says with
Jesus all things will
be possible. Some
day the children
ascend to be leaders.

Oil Paintings

a few candles burn
in the old church hang
massive antique framed
oil paintings from 1700
how is it the building
grows old and these
paintings stay the same
jesus mary and joseph
is it also moses and
god the father I am
not certain but what
a surprise in atlacomulco
to find some paintings
like those hanging at
the louvre the prado
or the art museum
in washington dc

The Caretakers

Wearing their beautiful
skirts, and blouses
they make at home,
they have their gray hair
in braids. Except a woman
with snow-white hair
who smiles, but doesn't
want to pose for her photo.
The women finish mopping,
and they go outside to
dump their water, and wring
their rags, then come back
inside to kneel and pray.

Outside five men
carry a forty-foot long
solid wooden ladder.
They put it up beside
the Cathedral front.
A man at the top
tosses a rope end down
from the steeple.
These are the men
who will ring the bells.
Now they try to clean
Mary's statue, who the birds
find useful for a nest.

In The Kitchen

Four women cook mission
breakfast at stoves.
Their radiant laughter
is warm as the fires
they use for cooking.
A calendar on the wall
and times moves slow.
A table and 13 chairs.
There is no metaphor
for the Holy Spirit.
With the grace of many blessings
the table set with
oatmeal, toast, tortillas,
papayas, apples, bananas,
eggs, meat, chili sauce,
beans, cheese and jello.
Delicious, with hot chocolate,
or tea made with camomile.
How is it you are here?

Dinner With the Mission Ladies

Three ladies, two are retired
nurses who speak a little English.
Another lady speaks only
Spanish, and it's not clear
what type of work she has.
She has been at the Mission
a few weeks. The ladies and
Rich, and me go into Lenis,
a restaurant like Denny's,
Saturday night, and we
sit at a booth. The ladies
sit together with the younger
one between the gray headed
nurses who chat with me.
Rich sits in his wheelchair.
I sit at the end of the booth,
the part that curves out.
Rich orders a burger and fries.
I order a strawberry shake,
and a club sandwich. The
Mission ladies order pancakes.
My shake turns out to be
strawberry milk, the kind
I haven't had since I was
a kid. My club sandwich
so huge I give half to one
of the nurses whose pancakes
look and smell delicious.

3039-PEAR

I ask Rich to translate
so I can talk with Martha.
I find out she has
raised a son, and never
been married. He studies
now to be a minister
at the University of Mexico.
And she studies too,
a course on Thursday
nights, covering
the first five Bible books,
the Pentateuch.
After dinner Rich can't
pay the bill because
his fifty dollar U.S. Traveler's
Checks are either too big
or unacceptable, so I foot
the bill with American cash.
Only I don't have enough
so Martha chips in for
the remainder in pesos.
Everybody we walk past
on the way out is smoking,
and the entrances are
curbs, or steps, so they
don't have handicap
awareness yet. Rich and
I hope to raise their
consciousness a little.
As we get in the van
Rich drives, and the older nurse
sits in the passenger seat.
There are only two seats
in the van. The other two
ladies are in the back

sitting on a cooler.
I sit on the floor across
from them. Martha has
sleek black hair and
deep black piercing eyes.
She is attractive, and smiles
at me and looks me in
the eyes the whole way
back to the hacienda. It's
a magical night. The stars
are beautiful, and Martha
points out the moon is an
orange crescent setting
over the mountains.
At the Mission the nurses
go to their apartment.
Rich goes to our place.
I walk Martha to hers.
We hold hands, and
kiss goodnight.

Lost In Mexico City

Rich drove through
Mexico city when
I asked him to
go around because
our destination
was Cuernavaca.
It was quicker to
take the country
road, but Rich drove
through the middle
of Mexico city on
Sunday when it was
a day with the least
traffic, but it was
awful, bumper to bumper
and stand still jams.
Our map was terrible.
Half of the streets
were not on the map,
and by the time
we realized where
we were, it was a one
hour drive east of
our turn south.
So we had to back
track and ask for
directions that we
listened to, but did

not comprehend.
The three hour
journey lasted
for six hours.

VW Heaven

all the volkswagens
died and went to
mexico reborn as
blue taxis in one
place green in another
then on the road
red orange yellow and black love bugs
slim sexy bodies easy on
the gas no dents no rust
they look brand new
polished and clean
waiting to take you
anywhere you say

Driving to Cuernavaca

At Atlacomulco irises bloom,
a mellow harvest moon
in an orange crescent shape
smiles down on lovers
under magnificent stars.
The mountain air is cool
on exposed skin.
On farmland near the hacienda
dry plants wear winter white,
or black patches, from fire.
Drive south in the morning
this is the most beautiful
route on the journey,
meandering through foothills
toward Cuernavaca, and you
have emerald clover fields,
haystacks, and leafy mature
tree boughs shading the road.
It might be Georgia with pines
covered in moss, or northern
California where redwood
trees reach up into clouds.
Coming into Cuernavaca,
is like a jazz saxophone
singing irish green and flowers,
into a city that looks out

over rolling hills, and narrow
cobblestone streets, with
joyful crowds of people
selling everything you want.

Cuernavaca

There wasn't
a cloud coming
across the sky
for the whole
trip. In fact
during my week
at Cuernavaca
it was comfortable
77 degrees.
Small streets
curved uphill
then over canyons.
I thought, I like
this place so well,
I might stay here
and write poetry
forever. Thursday
wild horses
rumbled thunder
in a stampede
across the grim
purple sky.
All night long
the soft rain
hummed on my
roof. By morning,
clouds have made
their quiet exit.

Washing Demetrius

At the Tola family home
there was a topless
candy apple red jeep
in the garage and a curly
medium size gray mutt
a street dog. I was a guest
with the Tola family a week.
Mr. & Mrs. Tola worked at
their metal engineering
business and Monica, their
28 year old daughter was
a TV reporter for channel 4
on the six o'clock news.
I watched her every night.
I asked her why her jeep
was topless and she said
because it never rains.
Monica had a soft spot
in her heart for animals.
She found Demetrius on
death row at the shelter
and brought him home,
a perfect companion
for her beautiful female
a pure golden retriever.

Demetrius was fun and
followed me on walks.
His curly fur was matted
and in a tangle. I asked if
I might wash the dog.
I had not washed a
dog before. I had washed
a car, or my laundry, but
not an animal. Mr. & Mrs. Tola
said Evie, their young
house maid would help.
So I filled a plastic washtub
with hot water and got my
Herbal Essences pink shampoo
with rose hips, and put those
in the backyard beside
the bird of paradise
that was about ready to bloom.
Evie brought more hot water
and I brought Demetrius.
We held him by the water,
told him to sit, but he was
a wise dog and had
been on the street so long
he could smell water, and ran
away barking. He was locked
in. I caught him. Evie poured
bowls of water on him as I
put a quarter of my bottle
of shampoo on him and
we both laughed while we
scrubbed and rinsed three
times until to our surprise
Demetrius was a white

haired dog. We rinsed him,
he shook spraying, then
I took out my Swiss pocket
knife scissors, cut the gum
and burrs out of his fur,
trimmed his bangs up,
you could see his big brown
eyes. I trimmed off his beard,
shaped his handlebar mustache,
and he looked like a different
creature. Monica later said when
she came home and called him,
as was her habit, he came up
whimpering, look what they did.
Then Evie and I washed the
golden retriever who did not
put up such a fuss, but ran
up the metal circular stair
outside and hid on the roof
while Demetrius was being
given his water torture. Her fur
shined like a fashion model's
hair and she was easy to trim.
She had a couple of furballs
matted on her long ears.
She shook when I unlocked
the garage door and they both
ran up the back alley barking.

Walking

In Cuernavaca I took morning
walks. Demetrius the curly haired
dog would come along for about
two blocks, then he would leave
me to walk in solitude. Bright
crimson and hot pink flowers
were blooming on the trees and
shrubs here. A tree with big orange
orchid like blossoms filled the sky
overhanging across the narrow
cobblestone avenue. Now a large
tree with lavender flowers and no
leaves at all, and flowers every color,
every variety, thrive so that my walks
were feasts for my eyes.

On the beach at the coast—
I had not seen the pacific
since 1972, or heard the roar
of waves curling toward sand.
I walked barefoot in the salty
white bubbling waters approach,
then in sand as it receded
in a timeless rocking rhythm,
and carried my aged leather
sandals. A lone dolphin

swam south as I walked
in the same direction.
I collected shells that were
too beautiful to pass by,
and watched the sunset.

Downtown

I walk past a private
school called shakespeare
where the young are
taught english
morning sunshine
enhances flowers
blooming everywhere
there is a bush or tree
lazy dogs sleep
on the walks content
I stop at the laundry
to find out how much
my clean clothes
will cost me and I
get directions to
the post office
I have six cards
to drop off there
I stop for a scoop
of chocolate ice cream
the hustle and bustle
adds character to beautiful
city streets where
a giant neon sign
flashes circles and
layers of light
advertising coca-cola

Jogging in Cuernavaca

I am the only person
here who is jogging.
I jog to the Zoo,
and ask permission
to run in the park.
I'm told to come back tomorrow
at ten when they open.
So I go up the main boulevard
in four lane heavy traffic.
It's not possible
to jog in the street.
The walk is narrow
there are people
everywhere, trees
grow in the middle
of the walk with
cracks, bumps and
other obstacles. No way
to go fast, when curves
and hills interpose.
So I jog up the sidewalk
for thirty minutes
not breathing deep,
air pollution. When
I see Cuernavaca
Plaza, I turn around
and jog home.

53 Chevy Pickup

Cherry red looking
like a new pickup
except an original
windshield has a crack.
Rubin Tola Jr. drives
over speed bumps
around a circular plaza
toward the family
business where
I watch his dad
and three workers
lift a metal frame into
a truck to be delivered
to a local factory.
Rubin wants
to know how
they can begin to build
wheelchairs because
few people in Mexico
are currently doing that
wheelchair access is a
problem also.
We drive back through
the circular plaza
and buy 24 red roses
for Isabel Tola, his
mother and my gracious
hostess. When Rubin

told me, "my truck is
your truck," I felt
like a kid getting
a ride on a fire truck.

The Gazebo

Sitting in the center
at a large glass table
every morning I write
page after page. Poetry
and journal entries flow.
The gazebo in the 'Tolas'
back yard is the perfect
place for writing.
In the lime tree robins,
and sparrows are singing.
Evie sings from the kitchen.
The garden has yellow roses,
and the bird-of-paradise
is beginning to bud.
I am amazed everyday
by the beauty of this
gazebo, and how much
I have written here,
and I think I would
really like to stay.

Shopping With Monica

My brother tells me
that before I was born
he recalls moving from
Ashland to a farmhouse
without any furniture.
I was the youngest, always
got more than they did.

Now in Cuernavaca Plaza
I meet Monica who has
come from her reporting
job at the TV station to
help me shop for new clothes.
And we buy navy blue Dockers
trousers, and a white shirt,
and go to another store where
only Pepe jeans from London
are sold, in fact, several
Plaza stores sell jeans.

Monica is very attractive.
Hers is that rare beauty
of a movie star. She takes
me into stores where
she looks but doesn't buy.

The mall is crowded with
young beautiful well dressed
women who shop in groups.

Later we go to a shop
and I buy socks, and
underwear, then we go
because later we will
have dinner at a fine
restaurant, and Monica's
mother will ask me if I
think Monica is pretty.
Now we are in her red Jeep
with the top off, flying over
speed bumps, zig-zagging
through traffic, on streets
lined with palm trees.
The balmy breeze was
blowing through our hair,
and the moonlight gave
a mood for romance.
And it would have been
like a date, shopping
with Monica, except
her mother was with us.

Speed Trap

A beautiful drive
through hair pin
curves in the forest
like driving up Flagstaff
mountain in boulder.
This scenic drive lasted
for a few hours. I went
around a tight corner
and there were several
green and white police
cars. The Federales were
in dress uniforms, white
shirts with official silver
trim and black trousers
with sharp creases. They
waved for me to stop.
I was going 15 miles per hour
well under the speed limit.
In very broken English
one of them took my
Colorado driver's license,
then said I would have to
pay a 500 peso fine for an
infraction. I asked what it was.
he pointed to a tinted window
on the rear driver side of
the 1978 white Ford van.
I asked for their Captain. He

was 65 miles in the opposite
direction. I asked him to show
me the infraction in writing.
He pulled out a booklet,
and handed me a paragraph
written in Spanish.
They couldn't see the window
as they motioned for me to stop.
I offered him 400 pesos.
He returned my License.
I was fortunate to have it back,
and I drove on, glad to be alive,
not murdered in a canyon.

A Sculptor's Song

Who worked on this metal?
How did they shape it into
stallions and buffaloes,
birds and abstract art, until
light, or color trick your eyes.
They worked with diligence.
A trained master has made
this hand stretch open,
a permanent lover's kiss,
and dolphins leap in space
where water fountains flow.
These Mexican sculptures
defy any description, except
to say, they are stationed
in the main intersection
on boulevards everywhere.
A giant historical figure,
or a thirty foot Jesus
in marble, and roses
on his wounded feet.
Wild stallions run faster
than break neck speed,
snorting and tails flared.
Weather corrodes these
fine works. They turn green,
while the guitar strums
the mariachi band plays.

Guadalajara

Arriving at sunset the Holiday Inn
wanted 100 dollars per night,
per person. There was a better
place for much less. The Bell
hop spoke English, and joked
with us about Rich's bad Spanish
sounding like he wanted a room
with seven white women in the room.
I had to remove the bathroom door,
and the shower doors so Rich could
get through in his wheelchair, then
we strolled up the avenue to the Crab
House, a fine food establishment that
occupied a whole block. Both of us
ordered the house clam chowder.
It looked like baby food, and had a
fishy odor. Rich had a beer, then Sunday
in the morning, he was sick. I drove
around a plaza with six lanes, and
stop lights, a dozen roads intersected.
Two Federales on motorcycles
pulled me over, and asked,
"Did you see the lights?"
For some reason I said, no,
even though they were green.
So I got out, slammed the door,
and started acting crazy.
I pounded on the lift doors,

and fulminated, "Emergency, El
Bano, Emergeny." The cop glanced
inside at Rich, who was sick,
shook his head, and revved
his Harley and rode away.

Customs

On the edge of Mazatlan
after driving for two days,
a young Mexican man
in civilian clothes waves
to pull off the road.
Rich was driving. I told him
not to pull off, but he saw
it was a check point.
He had to drive the van
over a ramp and they
inspected underneath,
then a guy who spoke
good English asked me
where we had come from.
I couldn't recall Guadalajara;
it didn't come to mind, and I
looked at Rich who also,
couldn't remember. I was
told to get out of the vehicle.
They were going to inspect
for drugs and I was taken
aside by the Customs man
who got in my face, and kept
repeating, "tell me where
the marijuana is now,
and I will be easy on
you later." At that point
my heart started pounding

and I felt like running, or
punching him, but I didn't.
I said I don't smoke, but
he had prejudged me on my
appearance. He knew I was
running drugs. I explained
I was a Boulder Road Runner
not a smoker, and showed
him the Missionary letter.
He said, "it was very nice,"
but started in with, "tell
me now where the marijuana
is, and I will be easy on you
later." Then he walked away
and motioned for us to
leave. As we did Rich
said he told them that he
didn't even like marijuana.

Mazatlan Tennis

It was the first
time I had seen
the Pacific in
twenty-six years.
It felt good
driving north
up the beach
beside joggers
stopping at the
best hotel to see
if a cab driver
friend had made
a reservation,
while the rich
American yuppies
were staggering
drunk in the lobby.
I was glad there
were no reservations.
Way up the beach
at Mazatlan Towers,
an expensive time
share, the luxury
condo was free.
Rich negotiated for
two days to coach
a wheelchair
tennis clinic

in the summer,
a very big deal
with Pro players
and TV coverage.

Mazatlan Towers

If you have $7,000
you can buy a time
share condo at the
Mazatlan Towers,
and stay there a
whole week for
the next 75 years,
or for 75 consecutive
weeks, or any other
combination, and
these condos are
luxury furnished,
and on the pacific.
Wealthy people
from other places,
Canada too, come
here for vacation,
sun and sand, to
hit the night parties,
for tennis, parasailing,
golf and horseback
riding, or moonlight
walks on the beach.
The swimming pool
a thirty second walk
from the ocean is
heated and olympian
size, for Greek Gods.

Food is served by the
pool, or in the restaurant
that is also a piano bar,
and a dance pavilion.
On the outside its
thatched roof rises
like a hidden missile
site, but inside it is
hollow, the back of
thatching. They tell
me it leaks when
it rains, but it rains
so seldom nobody
will notice. I am a
guest here for three
nights and two
days, then begin
to drive back home.
The thing that
troubles me
the most on
this trip bringing
wheelchairs into
a place where
nobody had
wheelchairs before
is the contrast
between wealth
and the poor
in Mazatlan.
Across the four
lane boulevard
is a poor family
left to scratch
their livelihood

out of the dirt.
As you drive
north out of
town, Mazatlan
Towers are there
beside the finest
group of new
buildings on
the beach, and
along the boulevard
a long line of palm trees,
then you have desert.

First Night in Mazatlan

Chips and salsa
in the afternoon
beside the pacific.
Wind blowing in
from the water,
sunlight sparkling
on the gentle swells.
Pelicans fly over.
I sip lemonade.
At the next table
two women invite
me to join them.
One woman just
flew in from Denver
an hour ago. She
wants to know
if I am single.
I watch the sunset
drop a golden eyelid
below the water,
then I go to the
Sol de Soul beach
restaurant for
dinner, and watch
an artist spray-
paint a colorful
space odyssey.
And I think kids

who paint graffiti
in America could
learn how to make
money from this
type of painting.
And later as I walk
along the balmy
avenue, I see
a man wearing
a dark business
suit, and he crawls
on the dusty sidewalk
because he has
one leg and cannot stand.

Sun of Soul

The best place
to eat on the
beach is a little
restaurant known as
Sol de Soul.
I went for dinner,
and ate delicious
chicken teriyaki
on the back terrace
where I could
see moonlight
on the pacific,
and listen to waves
crash the shore eight feet
away from my table. There
was one table row here so
on one side were
young sailors in
civilian clothing
chugalugging beer,
laughing, smoking cigars,
and at the other table
were two young women.
I sat there and enjoyed
the balmy ocean breeze,
and toward the end
of my meal, someone
began to shoot off

fireworks, over the
beach, and everybody
in the place came out
to watch the colors
explode on the water
like waves of rainbows.

Graffiti Artist

In the USA these guys paint walls for free.
A crowd gathered at a restaurant, and bar.
Vacationers here from around the world
in sandals, t shirts, cut off jeans, trying
to look like beach bums, or surfers with
cocoa butter tans, and sun bleached hair.
Joining Mazatlan night life, drinking, and
dancing, this crowd of wealthy onlookers
stood with their jaws dropping in awe as
they watched a graffiti artist. With his case of
spray paint and different sized plates, and tin
cans, in minutes paint unique planets, swirling
clouds, red nebulas, comets, with broad tails,
domed Star Trek cities, a desert, a lone tree,
a highway going inland, a mountain range,
moon craters, then add his flowery signature.
He sprayed over a cigarette lighter left out to burn dry.
Eagerly they gave big cash for his paintings, as if
they discovered Henri Matisse, or Pablo Picasso.
Fumes, flames, and alcohol, made them hot works.

Two Fish

A puffer fish appears washed up
on a rock another wave takes
it downshore it is flowing
in the tide dying too weak
to swim it was left way
up on the beach to dry.
I pick it up by the tail
put it back into the water,
and I watch as it swims
out on sparkling swells.
I walk along and wonder
why this cycle, then I watch
a sandpiper as it races away
when the next wave comes on
with bubbling foam.

I love wind
sun and salty
spray on my face
and I take a long
walk north on the beach.
After an hour I find a gutted
seabass, its scales made
a rainbow in the sunshine,
one hollow eye socket
one blank glazed eyeball

a magnificent fifty pounder
an old fish with powerful fins.
Overhead seven pelicans glide
on the horizon a majestic sailboat,
hot sand between my toes.

Lifestyles of the Rich and . . .

Famous, well not famous,
but rich. You know, it's funny
they don't think they are
rich. They think normal. She says,
"Darling we come here for
three weeks every February,
from Canada, You know, there's a
publishing war going on
there right now, and this
is my daughter. She's
blond and blue eyed.
Her daughter is Puerto Rican.
She lives there on a farm
I bought, but her husband
left her because he didn't
want to farm. She first came
down here with two girlfriends
from college. They drove down in
a Volkswagen bus. She said
she was afraid the border
patrol would stop them.
They had marijuana, but
they just waved them
through. Didn't even have
to stop, but the best thing
to do is offer them a
cigarette if they make
you get our of your car.

I interrupt her and ask—
where did your daughter
get that awful purple and
black, eye. She says, "it's the
funniest story, they were playing,
she and my grand-daughter and she
raised up and banged
her head against my daughter's
eye. When I came in to see, she
had this big ice pack
on her head, and says
she is seeing double.
Tells us to go to dinner
without her. It happened
last night darling.
So you see, her eye
is much better now.
Tonight at dinner she will
wear her new sunglasses.

For Honeymooners

Parasailing from
the beach they
go up fast until
they are a tiny speck
above the water and
they glide along
the shore behind
white breaking waves
hooked to an extremely
long tow line on a boat
and then return for
a gentle landing
in the hot sand.

Saddled horses
one paint, one red,
their galloping hooves
might be in rhythm
leaving a trail
of wet hoofprints
happily married
they carry people
that might be in love
and have their long hair
blowing in the wind
their wild smiles
spreading joy.

Everlasting the sun
shines down here
on natives who
ply their wares along
the shore they sell
shades to vacationers
in designer swim wear.
Where can you get
protection from the sun
at this price
for the same frames
worn by Hollywood stars?

The honeymooners wear
sunglasses, they have
sandals and leather belts
with silver buckles
and silver earrings
hand crafted, as
the natives say,
by a family member
they wear island hats
and lie on blankets in
a gold and purple sunset
they have true love.

Crop Dusting

On the drive from
Mazatlan the ocean
was on the left
and many beautiful
farms had green crops
in all stages of growth.
I saw six inch corn
and some knee high
and some with tassles
ripe for the picking
several small planes
flew low spraying crops.

This was the richest
farmland I saw in
Mexico. Along the
west to the border
there is a lot of poverty
and a common sight was
a donkey and wagon.
I saw one with a
pretty teenage girl
seated in the wagon
at a produce market.

The flight of planes
that were crop dusting
twisted and turned, rose
into the sun invisible
and peeled over the van.
Tree lines and million dollar
tractors plowing hearty fields
reminded me of farmland in
Southern Illinois.

Cattle and a Windmill

praying for peace
works better than
protesting

crossing the border
at nogales arizona

red dirt
a few yucca plants
some catttle
and a windmill

it is good to
be back home

where brown
cattle with white
faces are healthy

and the slow windmill
turns
        pumping pumping

Friday the 13th

We prayed to cross the border
in Nogales without any trouble.
I wore my new clothes
navy blue dockers
and white shirt.
The Mexicans waved
the van through.
The American Border
Patrol checked papers,
had a dog sniff for drugs,
then said have a good trip.
I drove hard through
Arizona. The right
front tire began to
shake at seventy mph,
but ran smooth at
ninety-five. Arizona
was hard at work with traffic
hundreds of busy truckers were
hauling goods to America.
We stopped in Albuquerque,
New Mexico for the night,
then a friend Charley
bought our breakfast at Los Alamos,
and gave me a Christmas present.
What a surprise on Friday the 13th?

During breakfast the bad tire was
replaced. It had two broken belts.
Fortunately we arrived
home at Boulder safe.

Marine Basic

in memory of John Montreuil

Phase One

Drill Instructor
in a Smoky the Bear Hat

He just got back from Viet Nam. His green eyes have
red flames in them. Staff Sergeant Butler, one of our
DI's, crams his lion chest out wearing gold wings; the
emblem of Marines who are recon men. Four in his fire
team dropped behind enemy lines by parachute to survey
the area, count Chinese officers, North Korean Marines,
and Viet Cong. He has old tales to tell raw recruits
lurking late until his lungs expand neck veins pop up
his cocoa butter tan face grimaces, "Get your ASS on
the yellow footprints.

Yellow Footprints

Comical yellow footprints.
Find a pair and stand on them.
The DI wants us to do that,
obligingly you find a place.

An hundred-fifteen pound DI
screams at a 300 pound recruit
wants him on the footprints too,
but the big guy challenges.

Two hard quick punches
to the soft stomach.
The bantamweight gamecock DI
wins, in the first round.

No gloating here. The big guy
on the footprints grips his gut.
It is past midnight
and a dozen DIs huddle.

We are not in uniforms yet,
and we do not know how to march.
Under starlight we stand silently
wondering what will happen to us.

This is humorous and serious,
when the DIs break we are ushered
single file and every recruit
passes through the door.

When it is your turn you are told
to quickly enter through the door
and sit in the first chair you find.
This all happens with blinding speed,

within the first thirty seconds.
Never again will you stand on yellow
footprints, but you will remember
their color for the rest of your life.

Barber Chairs

Clippers humming
a barbershop quartet.

In the tradition
a long row of chairs.

One style for all mirrors
a thirty second haircut.

For all those hours
and you have joined.

Receiving

After you sprint
from the barber chair
you come to a long counter.
Great shouting
down the halls:
what is your waist size,
your shoe size?
Somebody throws a sea bag
green socks fly at you
belts, T shirts, boxer shorts,
all the articles of clothing
you will need for the next 12 weeks.
If you get the wrong size
too bad, tough shit, wear them.

Then the herd
stampedes into a room
with cubical desks.
You are given a box,
take off your civilian
clothes, put them into
the box, and address
the box to your home.
This is your last chance
to get rid of any contraband,
guns, knives, drugs you may

have brought with you without
getting into trouble.
It is the last time
you will see that box.

Get your group shower.
Gold dial soap bars
five shower heads
blast steam, duck under,
lather up, rinse off,
get out, drip dry, try on
your new boxer shorts,
T shirt, green utility pants
and socks, black basketball shoes,
gray sweatshirt, put on your hat
grab your sea bag and run
out the door. Everybody waiting.

The sea bag on your shoulder
might weigh 60 pounds.
The DI wants you to
form four lines.
The tallest man
in front. The shortest man
in the rear of the line.
Now put your left hand
on the shoulder of the
man in front of you,
and lock your right arm
around the left arm
of the man to your right.
Now walk and stagger
like a million legged
caterpillar.

Nobody knows how to march,
but somehow you finally
reach your assigned quarters.

Metal bunkbeds, wooden footlockers,
pick a bed, put your sea bag
into the footlocker.
You are given two green wool
blankets, two sheets, a pillow
a pillowcase, and the soft spoken
DI demonstrates how
to make your bed with
military folds,
expects you to
make your rack
like that,
gives you ten minutes
to make your bed.
And when he returns
your rack made,
you will be
standing at attention
in your skivvies.

The angry
green and red eyed
Drill Instructor
comes in yelling
to get your covers off.
"Take off those covers,"
everybody starts ripping
blankets and throwing them
on the floor.
Angry DI throws people

on the floor, anybody
he can get his hands on.
Then he grabs a recruit,
pulls his hat off and says,
"ladies this is your cover
and you better have
those racks made
before the other DI
gets back."

Soft spoken DI
comes in. Your bed is made.
You are at attention
in your skivvies.
He checks arms, legs, backs
for bruises, wounds,
broken bones, to be sure
we are healthy,
then tells us to get in bed.
At the light switch
he says, "there are armed
guards outside the door
with orders to shoot anybody
that tries to escape,"
then he turns out the lights.
"Good night ladies."
It is 3 a.m.

First Night Floor is Deck

Nomenclature
in the Marine Corps:
hat is a *cover*,
bathroom is a *head*,
Drill Instructor is a *DI*,
and we have become *ladies*.

Thoughts swirling
in your brain,
you have lived through
a worse nightmare
than you ever
dreamed possible.

You asked for it.
You enlisted.
This is temporary.
This will pass.
What is the best way to survive?
Go through it. You will make it.

If you can call two hours sleep
a night. That first night
calm, silent, peaceful,
your eyes close, mind slows,
then you hear Gabriel
sounding his trumpet.

"Take What You Want
But Eat What You Take"

—sign on the chow hall

1
Nobody gets up this early,
not tough birds
not sea gulls.
Starlight at morning chow.

March in stand at attention
take your hat off
ignore the aroma
as you go in the door,
pick up a metal tray
sidestep, sidestep,
hold your tray out
for food you want.
Everyday the same
shit on a shingle.

Toast, chipped beef, gravy,
and eggs turning green.

2
In lunch line I am talking.
Have I forgotten my manners?
No, I am midwestern,
friendly to strangers
asking what is good
and where are *you* from
to the cook who sings
"*I want to go home*"
in his nostalgic Country
and Western falsetto.
When a guy in a smoky
the bear hat sneaks in
and says over my shoulder,
"Meet me after chow
at the duty hut, Private."

3
Dinner hour,
wait for the last man
to arrive at the table.
Drill Sergeant commands,
"Ready seat. Bow your head.
Pray. Now get out you're done."
We eat while standing in line
waiting to shove
our dishes in the
dishroom window.

They feed us well
liver and onions,
part raw with fine flour
part burnt, and steak
country fried chicken
mashed potatoes and gravy
peas, carrots, corn, lots
of veggies, cakes, breads
anything to drink
from the soda fountain
and as much as you want.
There are rumors the best
chow hall is in Kaneohe Bay
Hawai'i. On Sundays they
will charbroil you a steak
outdoors, cooked to order.

Always something new
on the Marine Corps menus,
but regular chow too
pizza and spaghetti
with angel hair pasta
a Wednesday special.

Old Corps Tales

Staff Sgt. Butler's Tale

The mean, green eyed DI said he was fighting in the Tet
and a Chinese officer pulled out his saber waving it high in
the air and led the charge against the hill Sgt. Butler
was defending. That officer was bigger than a Chicago
Bears linebacker, and he was all coked up, thousands of
screaming soldiers ran behind. When Sgt. Butler fired
he hit him in the leg, but the guy was full of cocaine so
he was unphased continued to run closer. Butler shot him
blowing away part of his arm. He kept running, and Sgt.
Butler did not believe his eyes. How could he still be
coming? When the Chinese officer reached a few yards off
Sgt. Butler pulled an illegal weapon made in the USA a
12 gauge shotgun and blew him in half.

The Recruiter's Tale

Devil Dogs, Leathernecks, Jarheads, a few names you will be
called if *you* join. The recruiter rocks back in his chair, takes
a Camel nonfilter, lights it, and inhales. Yeah, I enlisted,
and went to basic. It was tough. This was the *Old Corps*. During
rifle inspection the inspecting officer found a tiny grain of
sand, a speck, in the barrel of a rifle, and that poor devil
had his thumb shoved into the bore and the officer slammed the
M-14 bolt home, and crushed his thumb. Another Jarhead failed
rifle inspection, had to sleep with his rifle a whole week.
The way I toss the truth around, who would believe me? Most
recruits think I am using reverse psychology making up these
stories to try and discourage them from signing up. Being a
Marine is a 24 hour a day job. This is hard, when you sign up
nobody knows what will happen, Vietnam is hell. You might not
make it. Oh, you want to join. Sign right here. Three years
and now I want to send you to St. Louis for a test battery,
and your physical. If you pass we'll write to you, then 1
October report here, Springfield. You recruits will bus to
Saint Louis, fly to San Diego Marine Corps Recruit Depot, MCRD.
After your basic training is complete you'll be one of the proud,
the few, a Marine.

The Sergeant Major's Tale

A Lance Corporal was sent over to my office from the Chaplain
who had asked me to cut orders for the young Marine, and I have
over a hundred clerks working for me here at Camp Pendleton.
My office, the largest on base, my desk all the way to the rear,
we work in one large room. On the white board up in back in
alphabetical order, the list of every Marine Base in the world.
So the Lance Corporal comes in, stands in front of me, I ask
him to look at the board and tell me where he would like me
to send him. Well, he looks at the board, his eyes as big as
a parachute opening, and he says he is a Ground Radio Repairman
and he wants to work in an Electronics Shop. Since there is
one just two blocks away he wants me to cut his orders for there.
Why, he could get his things out of his locker and carry them
to his new job. So that is where I cut his orders. They put
him in charge of their Radio Battery Shop, then six months later,
I cut orders for him to the Marine Airbase Kaneohe Bay Hawai'i.

Junk on the Bunk

Inspection
all of your
possessions
on your bed.
exactly regimented
boots spit shined
brass polished, rifle
clean not a grain of
sand a loose thread
or a wrinkle.
All in order
by the book
you stand at
attention while
an officer looks
down the bore
of your weapon.
Breathe a sigh as he
and the DI walk away.
Happy to have passed,
but one recruit
the highest score
in all events
will win honors
get a promotion
a free set of dress blues,
and on Graduation Day
he will lead the platoon
carrying the guidon.

The Gates of Heaven are Guarded by United States Marines

—Marine Hymn

In training we are
being taught to
have clear vision
as the eagle, to have
sensitive hearing as
the deer, to detect
a scent as the bear.
Jet planes fly overhead
and land every 15 minutes
at San Diego airport.
It is quiet.
I rest on my back,
listen for the chime
of hourly mission bells
to ring their nightly beauty.
Across the bay, in the distance
lights shine on the coast.
Moving toward shore
pacific waves curl surf
uncurl and wash foam
along the beach.
The foam recedes leaving
clumps of rubbery seaweed.

Wild horses in the
saltwater spray.
A fragrance of
eucalyptus boughs.

Duty Hut

Knock three times
and the DI begins to bark,
"100 bend and thrusts."

In this exercise you
bend over touching
your hands, thrust
your legs into a push up
position, bring
your legs back and stand.

This is my discipline
for talking in chow line.

After 100,
"Sir, the Private is done Sir."
DI said
"You are a liar.
You could not have done 100
in that amount of time."

He wants to know my service
number, wants me to
do 2630426
bend and thrusts.

Covered with sweat
and sand
I am doing bend and thrusts.

DI sits with his
feet up on the desk
sips a Pepsi
barks out, "You can go."

Calling Home

An old salt
Staff Sgt. Baker
was calling cadence
marching the platoon
across the drill field,
that same field,
made famous by
Gomer Pyle.

In perfect step
a precision machine
75 men settled down
marching from the waist
making every turn
every heel strike
then Sgt. Baker
called, "halt stand at ease.

Platoon attention.
Any man that wants to
call home, fall out."
He marched them
a few yards away.
He told them it was a
reward for their excellent
drill. Sgt. Baker said,

"because you are from
the St. Louis area
face east, call as loudly
as you can, HOME HOME HOME."

We heard them shouting
"HOME HOME HOME."
We heard Sgt. Baker who said,
"No answer, I guess nobody
is home. Now get back
in rank. Platoon FORWARD MARCH."
Some of us had a good chuckle.

Watering The Grass

Sand sand everywhere
and not a blade of grass,

carrying water by moonlight
splashing we all go.

We go with our bucket
to the head,

as it is our habit
before bed.

Every square inch around
our quonset hut we water

watering the grass, the grass,
this imaginary grass.

Reveille

Usually came before sunrise
dress go to the bathroom
brush your teeth fall in
for role call, and march
to morning chow,
afterwards every day
we went back to our
barracks to rake the grass.

Sand, sand everywhere
and not a blade of grass.
Furrowed rows of wet sand
raked to imitate cultivated
midwestern cornfields,
as seen from a jumbo jet.

Every square inch around
our quonset huts we raked,
raking the grass, the grass,
this imaginary grass.

Never was any damn grass there,
but every night we water
and every morning we rake.
A part of their mind game,
and we laugh at this foolishness
and try to keep hope alive
because the grass died long ago.

Orders

Staff Sgt. Baker
everybody respected
his integrity.

He played the role
of the loving father.
With his heart

like gold, tried by fire.
In the eighth week
practicing rifle drill

after supper, after dusk,
Sgt. Baker halted us
gave the order, "at ease."

Told those of us that had
cigarettes, and wanted to
could light them up.

He began to shoot the
bull with us privates,
then he paused, and with

a tear in his eye, said
he had orders for Nam.
This was his last day

I have not heard of
or seen Sgt. Baker
after that evening.

Gaslamp

The smoking lamp is lit.
Form two lines facing in,
if you do not smoke
you are the designated ash tray
and must carry your bucket
up and down the rows
until the smoking lamp goes out.

The smoking lamp is lit,
always made me think
of the 1800's gaslamp street lights.
At night somebody had to light them;
come morning somebody put them out.
If you've got them light them up.
The smoking lamp is lit,
always made me think
of Jerome Rothenburg's
"All I want's a good five cent cigar."

The smoking lamp is lit.
The smoking lamp is lit.
The smoking lamp is lit.

Note, each year there are 425,000
smoking related deaths in the USA.
If we lost those Americans in battle
we'd decide to win, or withdraw.

The Wreck of the Hesperus

Are you the wreck
of the Hesperus,
or what? Have you
ever fired a weapon?

I have fired
a Winchester 12 gauge
hunting with friends
on Illinois fields.

I doubted if Marine green eyed
Butler the DI
had read Longfellow
as he took me by surprise

with his direct question
right after I had
come out of sick bay
with five immunizations.

Earlier we marched
in white tee shirts
past fragrant rows of
eucalyptus trees without

being told where we were going.
Marines do not have Medics.
Navel officers and Sailors
staff our sick bay.

Sailors hate Marine recruits and
they were not gentle
at immunization time.
The biggest guys all fainted.

Five shots at once
is a shock. We carried
the big guys out,
then Sergeant Butler

called me over to him
and asked if I was
"The Wreck of the Hesperus,"
had I fired a weapon.

He sent me to the back of the line
to take those five shots again.
A Marine went in, we marched
one step closer to the door.

Some Marines are carried out
with their arms streaming blood.
I do not think I can stand
five more shots, but I stay in line.

It is the game they play
with your mind, to find out
if they can break you,
or at what point you will not

follow an order. As the last man
in front of me went through the door
Sgt. Butler told me to, "get in formation."
In formation, I am the morning star.

The Marine Corps Band

Grandfathers and grandmothers
mothers and fathers and children
are in the grandstand watching
the United States Marine Corps Band.
Perhaps my wife, mother and daughter . . .
their lionhearted faces solemnly
looking over the long drill field.
Unfolding the flag at morning colors,
the sharp creases of red, white and blue
uniforms as if the flag had come to life.
The flag is the length and width of the band.
Rippling in the wind. Raised up the flagstaff.
As the band begins to play and march,
precision marching, rows turn inside
reversing while playing bright anthems
marching in opposite directions.
Soft resonance of our National Anthem
sharp drumbeat of Marine Corps hymn
moving quick step pace across the field,
brilliant military music grows softer
in the distance as they march away
and the visitor crowd disperses.

Drill Sergeant
and Recruit Chorus

DRILL SERGEANT
Sound off.

RECRUITS
Sound off.

DRILL SERGEANT
One, two, three-four.

RECRUITS
One, two, three-four.

DRILL SERGEANT
I don't know, but I've been told.

RECRUITS
I don't know, but I've been told.

DRILL SERGEANT
The streets of heaven are lined with gold.

RECRUITS
The streets of heaven are lined with gold.

Running

75 recruits ran
along the beach
in San Diego a slow
group moving in step
their DI jogging backwards.
Some recruit named
Gene Autry sang cadence.
"Amen" was his best.
Six, seven, eight miles,
sand sun sweat pacific,
I always kept pace,
clapped and sang along,
"Everywhere we go
people want to know
who we are
so we tell them
we are the Marine Corps
mighty mighty Marine Corps."

Steve Lowe

We were in Boy Scouts,
and High School.
He was a fun person
he drove God's own blue Chevy;
at the drive-in-burger joint
we talked through our car windows.
He was drafted. I enlisted.
When we got back
we would get together there
and talk about our experiences.
I was out raking the grass,
the third week of training,
I saw him march by in a platoon.
I ran to the end of the barracks
right beside him and
called out his name.
I saw him for the last time.
He was a casualty.
His name, Steve Lowe, forever
on that black stone wall—
the memorial in Washington.

Next to of Course
God, Country, Corps

Why me? Why the Corps?
I had something to prove
raised by my mother
a couple of fading ridged
images of dad in my memory.
I felt I needed discipline,
and I needed the Marine Corps.

Here was the whole spectrum of men.
There were fat boys and skinny boys;
there was the guy who swallowed a needle
trying to get out; there was the guy
who would shit in his bucket every night
who did get out. At the other end
of the spectrum, a couple of guys were
perfect at everything, and handsome too.
I fell somewhere in-between and when
Drill Sergeant yelled "Fall In"
I had my place, my own point of view,
I was a color in the rainbow.

In Scouts our Scoutmaster
Jerry Lowe, Steve Lowe's uncle
was a Marine Sergeant. At night
clouds floated past the moon
on a camping trip. I saw him

press his trousers under the
mattress on his cot over night,
then when he woke up
he had sharp creases.
He was my role model.

There were a lot of good
people who became Marines.
I did learn self-discipline,
and I found that real virtue
came from inside of you.

Fat Boys and Skinny Boys

At chow 300 pound boys
were paired up with
boys that were under 150.
The smaller always got
all of the fat boys'
potatoes, bread and cake.

I was always paired
with a heavy body and
mostly they were jolly
good natured guys,
the kind you would
want to have beside you
in battle.

One recruit was mean as hell
always mad at the skinny
boy that got to eat his
potatoes, bread and cake.
He growled and grumbled
was never really able to
do anything about his loss.

By the end most fat boys
had lost 30 to 40 pounds.
The angry guy lost 60
and got down to 240
so that all the Marines

that were happy graduates
from basic training
weighed 140 to 250.
A lean mean fighting machine.

Absolute Nothing

Sergeant Major, three stripes up
four rockers down with a star.

Master Sergeant, three stripes up
three rockers down with a bursting bomb.

Gunnery Sergeant, three stripes up
two rockers down with crossed rifles.

Staff Sergeant, three stripes up
one rocker down with crossed rifles.

Sergeant, three stripes up
with crossed rifles.

Corporal, two stripes up
with crossed rifles.

Lance Corporal, one stripe up
and crossed rifles.

Private First Class,
one stripe up.

Private,
absolute nothing.

These are the enlisted ranks
of the United States Marine Corps.

Each hash mark on the forearm
right sleeve is six years of service.

Gentlemen, we do not
salute these fighting men,

you salute
officers.

Mail Call

The only contact
you have with a
world outside of
Marine Corps Recruit
Depot San Diego,
you sit on the deck
around Gunnery Sergeant
Sentinella our
platoon commander,
he rocks back
on his chair calling
out the names of those
fortunate few who will
receive mail from home.
Pity the recruit that
receives a stick of gum,
he gets to chew wrapper
and all. If it is a pack,
Gunnery Sergeant Sentinella
makes him distribute it
to his friends, and they
also get to chew wrapper
and all. He was always
laughing, enjoying our
misery and the power he held.
Heaven forbid your sweetheart,
or wife, sends a letter with
sweet smelling perfume

because he rocks back
and rubs the letter in
his crotch, then calls
your name. He always sniffs
each letter until he finds
one that smells good and
smiles, and calls the Corps
the crotch says we are all
in the crotch.

A Marine is a Rifleman First

Marines at weapons training
have to learn how to assemble
and lock and load every weapon.
There are more than a thousand
sorry faced recruits gathered
from the third battalion. All
their lips have been sunburnt,
turned down at the corners
into a typical recruit frown.
On stage our instructor barks
out nomenclature, the military
names of weapon parts.
First he scares hell out of you
making you imagine an enemy wave
in black pajamas at midnight
running when your weapon jams
in the attack. Chaos. The lights go.
You have 45 seconds. Tear it down,
clear out the jam, and reassemble.
Total darkness in the lecture hall.
Now you know you will get
hammered when a weapon jams
in the field. In a fire fight
this rifle is your life.

I Fear No Evil

Helmet, bayonet, flak jacket,
camouflage jungle utilities,
the reality of what you get
twentyfive miles of force
marching, camping, eating cold
C rations out of the can,
crawling under barbed wire
fifty caliber water cooled
machine guns firing over
your head, so if you sit up
you get cut in half and you
crawl in the dirt on your back.
Or sick as a dog you wish you
would die after three days at
sea, rocking side to side, up
and down, rocking and rolling.
Or practicing a beach assault
six thousand Marines landing,
never so happy to set foot
on land, loving that good earth.
And resting during smoking lamp.
Most of these guys write graffiti
on helmets used for their pillow,
"even though I walk through the valley
of the shadow of death, I fear no evil,"
that's what's written there—
like a prayer for courage—
where they rest their heads
and snooze.

At The Head

With green socks
tied around my knees,
a towel, a shaving kit
in my hand, flip-flop
shower shoes, gray P.E. shorts
I am marching in my platoon
as we go to the head to
shit, shower and shave.
Each night the DI on duty
gives us ten minutes
for these three tasks.
While we shower we wash our socks.

Here are four urinals,
two rows of sinks
with mirrors,
two rows of toilets
an open shower room,
plenty of hot water.
This is our most important
competition because
if we have to go again
we must wait for an hour
after taps and miss sleep.
If we miss places when we shave
the DI will dry shave our face,
as we leave the head
with our clean wet socks
tied around our knees.

Corps Sculpting

Thoughts splinter
genesis is a woman
somehow planets were created
sunlight reflecting off them
a steady glow at night
at home some young teen-ager
is pregnant waiting for her good man
to come back from basic
and marry her in his uniform.

Red yellow blue
circle square circle
shapes and found objects
gathered under the western sky
velociraptor and giant insects
a centenarian land turtle
a sea turtle flying through space
the lone star of the Brigadier General
who is a fighter pilot
this corps sculpting
shines in the sunlight.

Hollywood Nightmare

A bad dream comes back
like a comet this nightmare
with a broad tail swooshing
across the stars bits of ice
streaming fire and the dream
rips through your brain like that
until you wake in a cold sweat.
What was the dream about you might ask,
well imagine you are a Marine recruit
at San Diego Marine Corps Recruit Depot MCRD.
You are standing in line at receiving
where people are screaming for clothing
sizes, and all types of clothing are
flying in the air at you, but you are
a Corporal discharged at San Francisco,
honorably, with a good conduct medal.
When in the nightmare you realize
you are back at the starting point
receiving a clothing issue, and going
through basic over, and over again.
And because your training takes place
in Southern Cal., all other Marines
refer to you as a Hollywood Marine,
and this is a Hollywood nightmare.
Comet with a broad tail swooshing,
what is your waist size you puke?

Peace

Marines all go to church
on Sunday there are services
papers signed at enlistment
determined the service and faith
of each recruit. If you were Jewish,
Catholic, Christian, nondenominational,
all have their own meeting time.
Those going to my service
march with me to the auditorium.
For one whole hour each week
the DI cannot yell anything at you.
Most recruits are falling asleep.
Some are snoring, it is hard not to.
Vigorous activities, you are pushed through
in one hour regimented blocks daily,
until you sit in the plush red chair
and listen to the monotone minister
whose words lull you to drowsiness,
and the chair swallows your consciousness.
If you manage to stay awake the irony
of the message is from Romans 14:19
"let us then pursue what makes for peace
and for mutual upbuilding." Marines are
all for that, then at Sunday dinner bell
some of those more devout Devil Dogs
growl, "pass the fucking pepper."

21 Gun Salute

Another high school buddy
fell in love and married.
His young wife became pregnant.
He was such a cautious driver
when she was in the car 45 mph
was as fast as he would go.
One day he was rolling along
at 45 mph when his car
blew a tire, the door opened,
his bride was thrown out
a wheel pinned her stomach.
She died in his arms.
He joined the Marines.
He volunteered for
three back to back
duty tours in Nam.
Now a 21 gun salute
will honor his
Marine burial.

He Was a Car Thief

He was good. He could steal a car in less than a minute.
He'd taken 15 cars when he got caught: the Judge told him
he could go to prison, or join the Marine Corps for six
years. He was the happiest Marine. He wore his uniform with
pride. The Corps straightened out his life, and he was
happily married. A tall blond man with blue eyes, a new
life and many new friends. Everybody was amazed to hear
his story.

So You Want Out

If you wanted
out of basic
training, out
of the Marines,
the DI told us
to get off base
wait until after
midnight, take a
blanket, when the
firewatch was at
the far end of camp
make a run for it.
Throw the blanket
over the barbedwire,
hop over, and you
are in downtown
San Diego, simple.

If the Shore Patrol
catch you they throw
you in the brig.

If you wanted
out of life,
out of this world
altogether, then

cut your wrists
up and down the
arteries and veins,
do it in the shower.

If the suicide attempt
does not work you
are going to sickbay
until you are well,
then back on the
yellow footprints
for training at
square one again.

Trying To Get Out

A Private
swallowed
a needle.

He thought
he could get out.

Thought the Corps
would let him go.

Our DI let him
lay in his bed
three days,

then sent him
back to duty.

Another Private

He used the
blanket method.

We never saw him,
nor heard of him.

He went
AWOL.

Relieving Himself

Late at night
he would
shit in his
bucket.

Recruits
in his hut
complained.

For a week
he shit in
his bucket.

The Corps
let him out.

Killing in 8 Seconds

In hand to hand combat
we are taught to kill.
Not only to kill, but
to demoralize the enemies
will to fight. Instead of
taking a prisoner, pull
out their eyes and crush
them on their chest,
send them back to their
friends to show what happens
if they get caught.
Or to kill somebody
in eight seconds, grab
the enemies throat
snap their larynx.
With that pulled out
you cannot breathe
and you suffocate.

The Firewatch Ribbon

That first night we were told not to go outside because
there were armed guards. They turned out to be recruits
wearing orange vests, carrying flashlights on firewatch
duty. They wake you at midnight and send you out to a post
to walk the beat a couple of hours, and they tell you to
say, "halt who goes there," to anybody that comes along.
The hard part is staying awake. Everybody in the Marines
during the Viet Nam era was awarded the National Defense
ribbon. It was the big joke that was called the firewatch
ribbon, earned by walking firewatch. In the Marines two
things were certain: you'll walk firewatch, and you'll
have a National Defense ribbon. Actually it was pretty
red and yellow, white and blue, worn above the rifle medal.
All other medals, Purple Hearts, Bronze and Silver Stars,
were combat earned. An unusual moment in time, firewatch.

Famous Marines

Walt Disney proudly
displayed his Dishonorable
Discharge on the wall
of his office behind him
when he talked on his show.

Steve McQueen stole a tank
painted it pink and drove
down the main street in Oceanside
and they gave him a Dishonorable.

John Wayne played the role
of jarhead in the movies
a real Hollywood marine
he was so well loved
real marines idolized him.

Rumors

We were sitting around
on our footlockers
spit polishing our boots
cleaning our rifles
and writing letters home
when Staff Sgt. Butler
came in and said that
Paul McCartney of the
Beatles was dead,
sending shock waves
of depression through
us all. First John Kennedy,
Bobby, Dr. King and now Paul.
When would it ever stop?
Sgt. Butler said the papers
only had rumors. He was
barefoot on the album jacket
while the other lads wore shoes,
a symbol of his death, and nobody
knew exactly where he was.
Newspapers, magazines and TV
stations had the same rumors.
Paul McCartney of the Beatles
rock and roll band was dead.
That night we were all sad
when the lights went out;
our hearts were listening
when the bugle sounded taps.

Private in Another Platoon

Never bothered him
when the DI would call
him names, yell in his face,
or say that he was the worst
recruit they had ever seen
or heard tell of, he never
showed them any fear at all.
They pulled him aside and took
him out behind the duty hut
and asked him why he never showed
any fear when they started in
screaming and threatening him.
He said, "it was just like
being at home, Sir. Just like
the Private's home life."

The DI asked him to pretend
he was afraid and to play
the game because he was bringing
down the whole system. Couldn't he
just fake it a little? And then,
they sent him back and left him
alone after that, except when
they caught him talking to another
recruit when he should have been
cleaning his rifle. They beat him up
and he promised to return the beating
if he ever saw them again after basic.

You have to keep your rifle clean
in order to hit the target at the range.
It is important to qualify as Marksman,
Sharpshooter, or Expert.

Lewis B. Puller, Lt. General

Jupiter has four moons
discovered by Galileo.
Chesty Puller has five
Navy Crosses, the second
highest medal awarded
to a Marine.

Chesty fought four wars
and other battles
where U.S. Marines landed.

Once when surrounded
by an enemy he told his men,
"those poor bastards, they've got
us right where we want them."

An Army battalion
lost half their men
fighting through to them.
When he showed their officer
the line on the perimeter
to attack

their officer asked
where the troops
could fall back
if they were overrun.
Chesty got on the radio

to his artilleryman,
"if they move back a foot
shoot them."

Dog-eared

There was something
romantic about the Marines.
A book I'd read about leathernecks
at the battle of Peleliu
I found captivating.
Chesty Puller was C.O.
in one of the bloodiest
battles on a little island
in World War Two, then Captain
John N. McLaughlin was awarded
the Silver Star for gallantry
there. He later became Major General,
our Commanding General, at Marine Corps
Recruit Depot, where we were trained.
Robert Leckie wrote his book
from his personal experience
the book was titled *A Helmet
for my Pillow*; my friends
read, passed around and around,
until that book was dog-eared.
And I read the book last
I know this because I kept it.
I treasured that paperback.
There were wounds, pain and malaria,
we read the book at MacMurray
College's student union. Our
local high school hangout.
The Esprit de Corps first
touched me in that place.

John N. McLaughlin, Major General

The Commanding General. Once in a while we would see his car go by from the drill field. We knew it was the Commanding General by those red flags with two gold stars riffling on the wind as he whooshed by; it was not until later we would find out that he fought gallantly at Peleliu, and that in the Korean war he was held captive three years by the Chinese. When finally released he was awarded the legion of merit given for exceptionally meritorious conduct. During peace time he excelled in several positions stateside, and he earned a Master's Degree in International Affairs at George Washington University. By 1967 he was C.O. of the 6th Marines, 2nd Marine Division and was promoted from Colonel to Brigadier General earning a Gold Star in lieu of his second legion of Merit—while in Viet Nam—he became the Assistant Division Commander of the 1st Marine Division; he was promoted to Major General September 1969 and assigned to MCRD San Diego as Commanding General. I arrived there a raw recruit standing on the yellow footprints October 1, 1969.

Phase Two

_____

Edison Rifle Range at Camp Pendleton

Up until now we carried our rifles on the drill field. We learned how to do left shoulder and right shoulder arms, parade rest, salute, and in general how to tear down, clean vigorously, and reassemble our rifles. When we got to Edison we had classes on how to hold, sight and fire the M-14 weapon. This was the most important part of training. In battle that weapon would keep you alive. You needed to know how to fire and there are three medals for recruits who qualify at the range. This two week training period divided men, who would be Marines, from boys. Your first medal: Marksman, Sharpshooter, or Expert awarded. In two short weeks *you* would be tested; *you* would fire your weapon at the range. The totals, hits and bullseyes on the target would determine if you qualified. "If you do not qualify—you had better give your soul to God, because your ASS belongs to me," our Drill Instructor threatened, and he was serious this time. The third phase of Marine Basic is hell for recruits who do not qualify. Remember, a Marine is a rifleman first.

Intimate Dust

Fresh born like ducklings
eleven following their mother-hen,
we hike a dirt trail
following our Drill Instructor
in two columns with M-14 rifles
slung over our shoulders.
At the range we form a giant circle
for snapping in, or getting into shape
for shooting. We stretch
and take different positions
hours and hours we practice
prone and sitting, in the dirt,
intimately holding our weapons
with the straps around our hands, the
riflebutts tight against our shoulders
looking down the cold barrels
at the sights, and at the
imaginary targets, that poor slob,
the recruit opposite us in the circle.
This is the wild wild west.
The Pacific coast in the background
buzzards with their six foot wing span
circling overhead, rising in the heat.
By 21:30 I'm in the lower bunk
because at the range our day begins
at 03:30. Every muscle and
tendon ached as taps played.
DI turns off the lights, the sky

twilight, an arrival of stars
as we sing deeply the Marine Hymn,
and say our prayers, and go to
sleep. Our whole platoon in one room
with row after row of bunkbeds
in the new barracks. Our DI, spitpolished,
in his best dress uniform, rifle medal,
ribbons, recon wings, a killer smile,
going out for his night of liberty.

Snapping In

Pain is good
no pain, no gain
pain is impurities
leaving the body.
Circles of circles
get up at three-thirty
eat morning chow
hike to class
at Edison Range.
Most Marines in
the Japanese theater
during WWII had this
same training course.
We have our friend the M-14.
We have our shooting jackets.
Seated at the outdoor bleachers,
we are listening to instruction.
For a whole week
there are circles,
lying, sitting, standing,
stretching muscles
we did not know we had,
before stretching.
Hour after hour
seven days of snapping in.
Try to enjoy the silence
because next week
we'll have live ammo.

We'll shoot at circles
on targets 500 yards away,
then we'll shoot
to qualify for a medal.
Right now, impurities
are leaving the body
no pain, no gain
pain is good.

We Are Elements of Stars

Those stories you have heard
about Marines cleaning bathrooms
with toothbrushes, and the commander
checking places for dust
wearing a white glove, checking
ledges above doors, and pipes
and air vents, or a DI bouncing
quarters off bunkbeds to see if
they were made with military folds,
all of it is true. They made us
get up by 3:30 a.m.
to clean the head until it sparkled
to clean the floors to make our beds,
and then go to morning chow,
then hike to snapping in class.
We marched to chow in pitch dark.
The great thing was we could
see the stars at four a.m.
I could see the Milky Way
galaxy with thousands of stars.
A cloud of stars perfectly clear;
we are made of the same elements.

Outstanding

Liver and onions
are what we had to eat
for dinner.
The pressures here
were more relaxed.
The emphasis was on
learning to shoot accurately,
running and meticulous
cleaning of the floors and heads.
During our free time
in the evening we could
write letters home,
or shower and shave. I was
leaving the shower last
holding my shaving kit
in one hand, holding
a towel around my waist
with the other
standing there in my flip-flops
when the bantamweight DI and
my DI Sgt. Butler came in
and halted me
to play a little game
punching me
to see who could knock me back
further. I braced when they punched;
they both hit me three times.
Neither was able to knock me back a step.

They said I was outstanding.
Our showers were on the same
floor as their office,
and a glass wall divided
them from our living quarters.
Was I fortunate
to keep my liver and onions down?
The center of my chest turned scarlet.

Marksman

Would there be hell to pay
if you did not qualify
at Edison Rifle Range?
Not really. There were
over twenty recruits
in my platoon who failed
to qualify with the M-14,
the weapon of WWII. We had to
learn that weapon first, although
what we would use in Viet Nam
was the M-16 affectionately known
as the matty-mattel a plastic stock.
Recruits who failed in Marine Basic
they were yelled at a little more,
given work detail a little more,
expected to do better
in every Marine area
a little more, while
those of us who did qualify
could relax and celebrate because
we had earned our first medal,
and were we cool, or what?
A few had earned Marksman.
That medal was affectionately
known as the toilet seat.
Then there was Sharpshooter
a medal that was a Silver Cross.
The best was Expert rifleman

represented by crossed rifles.
These medals were worn
only on the dress uniform
directly below the National
Defense ribbon. You might be curious
as to which medal I received,
mine was the toilet seat.

Running Test

There are gentle rolling
foothills in California
wide spaces open for runs,
and our platoon goes out
for long slow group running.
Private Kennedy carried
our crimson pennant 3183
with a white flag below
with a black panther leaping
and these words, "Sent From Hell."
We go on runs of seven,
eight, or nine miles.
These runs most everybody
looks forward to for exercise,
and we go for morning,
afternoon and evening runs.
In step running side by side,
singing, chanting, clapping,
the DI running backwards
watching us go forward.
In boots, long pants, and
white tee shirts, through
the dust, and the sand.
Down through history
and time disjointed, what
position, like so many before,
and those to come afterwards
to the running test alone.

Running from one post to
the other, two hundred yards
away and back, timed for three
miles through dust, and dehydration.
No quitting, no stops, no resting,
no water for my parched throat,
just running. And mentally to
get through it, the whole way
I sang "Hey Jude" because
back at home the girlfriend
who waited for me was Judy.

Qualification Day

I am a small fighter.
There is a big evil
out there. How can we
stop the evil of our
time with bullets?
Our DI said if anybody
was nervous about firing
at the range he had
some tranquilizers,
gave out two per shooter.
They were gray pills
I popped them into
my mouth and chewed.
They were charcoal
placebo, placebo.
They stuck in the throat.
When it was my turn to shoot
I sighted the bullseye
and began squeezing
the trigger, and no matter
how tight I held the weapon
it pushed my shoulder back.
I squeezed. It pushed.
I knew the kick of firing
from hunting in the Illinois
winter fields with friends.
I had a 12 gauge Winchester
pump action shotgun that

fired three rounds before
reloading. I'd learned
how to hold a rifle against
my shoulder, how to hit
swiftly moving wild game.
These were stationary targets.
I could take my time,
sight and squeeze the trigger.

Saltpeter

Three days nobody in my platoon would eat butter. The rumor
going around was they put saltpeter in butter. Why did they
put saltpeter in our butter? Well, it would prevent us from
getting an erection. We would not want 75 horny 19 year olds
running around. After three days we ate butter. We did not
have radio, TV, VCR, no girls, except in our dreams, eating
was the pleasure they couldn't take away. Our rifle Instruc-
tor told us this rhyme while holding a rifle and his crotch,
"This is my rifle, this is my gun, this is for pleasure, and
this is for fun."

At Midnight

Rainfall is rare
in southern California.
Eight feet high fog
comes in from the Pacific
ocean, crosses the drill field,
then lifts into clouds.
Over my Marine raincoat
I have my orange vest on
because this is my night
for firewatch duty, and
I have a flashlight. I am
walking at midnight.
Streets, rooftops, palm trees,
eucalyptus trees, are wet.
Everything is wet or damp
from a fine mist in the air.
I am comfortable, dry and warm.
I can see the San Diego lights,
the bridge over the bay.
The muse is here with me.
We share this solitude,
and the fresh eucalyptus
on the sweet rain.

The Top Ten Things Marines Love and Hate

#10
Marines love being
in a large group of men,
they hate not being able
to see any beautiful women.

#9
Marines love being
immersed in their work,
they hate not being able
to go fishing, or watch sports.

#8
Marines love laughing along
with humorous mind games,
they hate being
the butt of the joke.

#7
Marines love wearing
their uniforms with pride,
they hate final inspection day.

#6
Marines love receiving
mail from loved ones,
they hate getting cookies, cupcakes,
and gum, and having to eat them
wrapper and all.

#5
Marines love being alive,
they hate dying in battle.

#4
Marines love being healthy
not getting the flu, or malaria,
they hate getting five
shots at a time from Navy Medics.
Shots make them faint.

#3
Marines love listening
to their Drill Instructor's voice
singing cadence at close order drill,
or telling salty combat stories,
they hate when the DI screams
commands at them barking like a dog.

#2
Marines love to eat mashed
potatoes and gravy, corn-on-the-cob,
peas and carrots, fried chicken, pork chops
and steak, cookies, cake and bread,
they hate when somebody skinny
is permitted to sit beside them
and eat their food.

#1
Marines love graduating from
Basic Training, and they hate that training
has ended that they will not see their
DI in his smoky the
bear hat anymore and wish they
could do it all over, "Go back and
DO IT OVER."

Sunflower and Moonbeam

Twelve weeks seem an eternity
when you are nineteen in Basic
if your girlfriend at home
is pregnant waiting for you,
misery is spending twelve
lonely weeks for the first time
being away from Judy miles apart
and recalling how cute she is
and the sound of her voice when
she would offer, "don't get mad,
get glad," from a pop TV commercial,
and time carries on a frail twig
in an angry river washing downstream.

Knowing not the future
the outcome of that moonbeam love
the sunflower of all the wonderful
days to come full of joy,
knowing not that at forty-six
love might have been something
you did not know you had and
twelve weeks seem a blink
of the eyelash, a wisp of fog.

Light raindrops on a windshield
diamond quality of light
passing through those raindrops
and the gentle sound of soft rain

when were together in the car
in front of Judy's home and we
had to say good-by not wanting
to be separated, that precious moment
etched permanently on my heart,
our daughter Crystal growing strong
and beautiful inside her mother.

3039-PEAR

Purple Hearts

After you are wounded in action
you are awarded the Purple Heart.

George Washington
his image is on the medal
in the heart shape,
the ribbon is purple.

Some I have known
received the medal and
will not speak of it.

Carefully if you listen
you may hear,

"a scar on the leg, shrapnel."

In Marine Basic Purple
Hearts are not awarded.

Anybody who went to Viet Nam,
their life was changed forever.
Friends who were casualties
they were awarded Purple Hearts.

Avoiding conflict,
how many went to Canada?

Sharpshooter Kisses

I am proud to wear
the Silver Cross on my chest,
the sharpshooter medal.
I am that Marine wearing it
on graduation day.
You know me.
I have seen the eagle fly
in the clearing
along an august marshmallow cloud
gliding the thunderstorm's edge
curve on the wind
then circle back.
In high country
along a fresh ice-melt river
I have stalked a moose
and seen buffalo.
When I fire my weapon
at the rifle range
qualifying day
I adjust for wind,
the minute inaccuracy
in the sight.
When I squeeze the trigger
lead flies like an
eagle in the clearing.

Expert Marksmanship

He is the best
at the range.
He hit center
never far from center
with each shot.
He will be the Marine
you want on your fire team.
He is the guy
you want beside you
in blazing battle.
On his chest
tiny silver crossed rifles
the best shooter.

Perfect sight
and precise
impact on target,
did you every
wonder with all
those recruits
firing at once—
how do you know
whose bullet
hit which target?
Just a thought.

I requalified,
went from marksman
to expert, although
I didn't feel
any different,
wore those crossed
silver rifles
with pride.

Twilight Hymn

Starlight begins to prick holes in the dark. And night
has its own light in that dusk purple sage. Its the final
skivvies inspection before bed at Edison Range, and all
the nonquals, Marksmen, Sharpshooters, and the Experts
are snug in their racks. Staff Sergeant Butler leads the
cattle lowing caterwauling of the Marine Hymn. The sound
of it is beautiful. Tomorrow, early we'll be on our way
back to MCRD in San Diego. By noon in the blistering sun
we'll march in close order drill across an asphalt surface,
heat falling in light on us like pollen off a sunflower.

Phase Three

Keeping Busy

The Drill Instructors are calling us Marines for the first time. We are allowed to wear starched and pressed uniforms with collars unbuttoned at the top, and our trousers bloused at the top of our boots. We feel and act sharp like Marines as we go into the final stretch of basic advanced recruit training. I am glad to have qualified as a marksman at the range. The DI seems to focus less on those who earned shooting medals and more on those who did not. These are the final preparation weeks polishing for graduation. Every hour in training is planned and structured. With diligence we work toward graduation day.

What is a Marine?

Marines laugh, cry, sing,
they raise families,
care about humanity
and want everlasting
peace in the world.

A Marine believes in
the United States,
is willing to stand up
and defend the country.

Is it a brotherhood,
a fellowship? Is it
not being willing to
leave anybody behind
in a firefight?

Many have taken up the
title of United States marine
and given their lives
for your freedom.

Men and women too,
that bled bright crimson
if they got wounded.

During a war or
a national emergency
if Marines are not
the first to go
then who is?

They are the President's own
ready for deployment
with 24 hour notice
anywhere on land, on sea,
and in the air

Sand Crabs

Where clouds billow along the beach,
you might observe a sand crab
run sideways into foam,
or hear the gull cry.

"I don't want to see you."
Our Drill Instructor was flustered.
We had all been out of step,
and out of line. That was
the absolute worst we had marched,
in close order drill, since
that first week in boot camp.

So the DI marched us into the sand, sand
consisting of sediment bits
with rough jagged edges,
and shell fragments.
This was a test of our true mettle.
This was humbling.
On our back with our rifle
we had to lay down
and bury ourselves in the sand.

Close Combat

Helmets and pugil sticks
were the great equalizers;
no matter what size you were
nobody could really get hurt.
A pugil stick
was like a giant
cotton swab with
padded gloves
to protect the hands.
We formed a circle in the sand.
The people in the circle
cheered, laughed and
whistled at the mortal combatants.
We had taken our covers off
preparing to put the
white football helmets on.
Here was the shiny skin,
our nearly bald heads.
With a DI on each side
it was kill or be killed.
Everybody had their turn
to attack an opponent.
When my turn came for close combat
I ran forward, screaming
as loud as my lungs would allow,
holding the pugil stick
like a knight's lance.
I caught my opponent

under the chin and
used my legs to thrust
upward as hard as I could.
He was knocked on his butt.

Grunts

Although every Marine
is basically a grunt
that's not what you join for
its what you get.
Drab faded olive green stuff.
Canvas backpack, camouflage
half tent shelter, a belt
with rifle magazine holders,
canteen, bayonet sheath and
bayonet, rifle, and a helmet
also in camouflage, virtually
all you'll need to survive
in the heat of battle and be
a grunt. A member of a team
of guys with mental and moral
qualities dating back to
November 10, 1775. Guys who
are always faithful and use
Semper Fidelis as their motto.
There's a famous monument of
the guys in green, the green
machine, guys raising the
American flag together at
the battle of Iwo Jima.
A grunt has tenacity of attack,
courage and faithfulness.
Some have tattoos of bulldogs.
Grunts are self-sacrificing,
always ready to keep peace.

Final Inspection

Our Gunnery Sergeant Sentinella
is in his full dress uniform
carrying a sword in his right hand
the blade facing forward
the blunt part resting
against his right shoulder
the most stern look
on his face tells us that
this inspection is serious.

Our platoon is aligned
into four squads or lines
in our dress greens
our buckles, shoes and
hat brims polished to
a mirror perfection.
At our right leg our
inspection ready clean
rifle. We stand silent
at attention. Waiting
for a Lieutenant colonel,
a First Lieutenant to
inspect uniform and rifle.

When the Lt. Colonel steps
in front of me, I snap the
rifle up diagonally across
my chest. When he makes a motion

to reach for my weapon I snap
my hands down sharply to my side.
This is the way it is done.
He looks down the barrel
for the slightest speck
of dust or sand, checks
the wooden stock and hands
the weapon back. Now he looks
at my uniform for a loose fit,
thread, or anything out of place.
"Outstanding Marine," he says
turning crisply to the young
man standing next to me.
He grabs his rifle. I breathe
easier. I passed.

Sergeant Neno
and the Samoan Sergeant

Sergeant Neno was a popular guy.
He loved the rank of Corporal
because with it came the privilege
of being a noncommissioned officer
without most of the responsibility.
Sergeants had to chat with officers
a lot and pass orders and instructions
along the chain-of-command to the men
of lower ranks below him. Sergeant Neno
did not care for that so every time
he was promoted to Sergeant he would
go to Waikiki beach and vacation there
for a couple of weeks. When he returned
he would be busted to Corporal.

The Samoan Sergeant had snow-white hair.
He had been in the Marine Corps
all of his adult life. He was the
most decorated Marine in WWII, or
so the story was told around base.
He had the Congressional Medal
of Honor and a chest full of ribbons.
He was a Sergeant and an alcoholic.
He was the linen room Sergeant.
A one man job. He took your dirty
sheets, when you brought them,

and gave you two clean sheets.
Every day he drank a six-pack
of Primo for lunch, then on his
way driving home drank another
six-pack of beer, then during
the evening drank two more six-
packs. A case of Primo a day.
He had been busted to Private
several times and would dry out
and work his way back up to Sergeant.
They would never throw him out
because he was a battlefield hero.

Last Hour of Sunlight

At dinner on the last day
of basic I finished early,
went outside the chow hall
to stand, and wait for
the other fellows to finish
eating their dinner.
It was the last hour of
sunlight. The time of day
when sunlight comes at you
from the west, and seems
to wash all around you
leaving a shadow that is
sixty feet going east.
There are three large
chow halls here in a row.
I am alone in the wide open
space. In the cloudless
western sky, a few sea-
gulls hang around for scraps.
This is the first time
I have seen a seagull
up close. The bird
walks right in front
of me, and stops to look
me over. The bird must
think it odd that I am
here all alone, and wonders
if I have any food. When

there is no food the bird
flies to the roof on the
chow hall. Soon a few other
fellows join me standing
in the light. With everybody
here Sgt. Butler calls us
to attention. We turn, "right
face," and begin marching . . .
left foot first, right,
left right, left right, left
right, away from the chow hall.

From the Halls of Montezuma

This is a black and white photograph.
One of the buildings that surround
the drill field. A receiving barracks,
they were all the same with pale yellow
exteriors, and red tile roofs, and halls.
You could walk down the halls like a
porch, and be outside the building, yet
underneath the roof looking ahead.
It was like walking through the halls
of time knowing everybody came into the
Corps and had a similar experience,
a similar feeling. Treasures from home
were lost. Childhoods forever left behind
in material things: baseball card collections,
coin and comicbook collections, bats, gloves,
high school letters, all the mementos
your childhood could gather, including
youthful, smiling friends, were lost.
If you survived, then you would be
a man. There were trees around my homeplace:
an ancient tree-of-heaven, a mature maple,
a gold apple, and a flowering catalpa
that a catbird called home. In the summer
there was a row of peonies and splashes
of colorful tulips in the spring.
And brilliant friends, all had to be left.
You had to look less at the material world
walking down those Marine Corps halls

that black and white photograph,
and ask what was to gain from the loss?
Sometimes a person has a long, long,
amazingly humble walk.

Faces

What do we know
we can take away
from Marine Basic?
Those first two weeks
were orientation.
The DIs tried to scare
us, tear us down, and
put the fear of God
in us, as we became
familiar with the
place and faces.
When it is ended
and we are Marines
working our eight
to five jobs, and
beyond, when we go
back to civilian
life many years
from now, what
will we have
memories of? Faces
with down turned
lips, burnt by
the sun and wind.
Faces that blend
and run together,
a few names
an image here

and there.
The DI
stands alone
adjusts
his cover.
He is waiting
for his next
platoon of faces
to arrive.

Unrest

Inside indoctrination;
outside race riots
and protests anti-war
demonstrations
blood on the gates
citizens beaten by
Chicago police,
the National Guard
shot its own citizens,
students at Kent State.
Outside you have
drugs, alcohol, tobacco.
Inside you have
tobacco; it was killing
us. And we had political
parties spying illegally.
Free love, free sex,
the Beatles were
disillusioned, went up
on a rooftop to make art
by playing their last gig
together, a free concert.
Men walked on the moon.
The flag unfurled,
silk gossamer, waving
in the wind, and the
tides unchanged, went out
and came back in, went

out, and came back in.
And nobody knew what
to do.

Marine Ball

The men wear the same
white hat with a gold
eagle, globe and anchor.
A nehru jacket so deep
navy blue that it looks
black. With gold buttons.
Bright blue trousers with
a wide red stripe
down the outside seam.
Shoes spit polished black
with high gloss.
A stainless steel sword.
The women beautiful
in dinner dresses of
different styles and
elegant colors.
That is what you join for
floating to the music
across the dancefloor
still a contender and
the band plays on every
November 10th, on the
Marine Corps birthday.
Like a harvest moon
floating through clouds,
hung on the ceiling a
ball made of mirrors
spins the light around

and around the floor in
the dark and the music.
A couple goes outside
to sit on the porchswing,
you and your bride-to-be.
A moment they look at
the orange moon, they kiss,
love comes back like love can.

Dreams That Shapeshift

Point blank I knew a Marine Corporal
He went to Electronics School after basic
in San Diego for a whole year.
He thought he wanted to be a
Secret Service Agent, take a
correspondence course in sociology,
the prerequisite for criminology.
He got orders for Hawai'i, tried out
for their fast pitch semipro softball team.
Marine bases had their own teams.
He made the next-to-the-last cut,
began to dream about the big leagues.
It was fun. He was hitting the ball
to the fence and he couldn't believe it.
Also, he was catching balls in center field.
The team was going to keep two players who
would be expected to purchase their own
uniforms. He made the final cut, then
he got sick. He did not buy his uniform,
nor did he play baseball. In the hospital,
they kept him for observations.
After his kidney surgery was successful
he went to work in the Urology Clinic.
I heard he attended Illinois University
majored in anthropology, and writing.

What Were The Three Hardest Things About Marine Basic?

Getting into shape. In the beginning my weight was 115. At the end, after twelve weeks, my weight was 140. Three square meals and regular workouts helped me to gain weight for the first time in my young adult life. If you were an Ohio State college football player, you might be in worse shape after basic because training was not as rigorous as NCAA weight training. The first weeks the USMC tore us down, then they gradually built you back up, but that was never an easy process.

Doing exactly what you were told. Turning left when commanded to and striking your foot down when everybody else did in close order drill with a rifle may look easy, but it is not. Then you were given ten minutes to shit, shower and shave. It became a competition. There were twenty-five toilets, four long urinals, eight shower-heads twenty sinks and you had to learn to go in shifts.

Being away from home. No contact from the world outside, without any comforts of home except for an occasional mail call and reading the Sunday paper was hard. Also, being isolated from family, friends and those you love was hard because in Marine Basic there were no phone calls, no TV, movies, VCR, or girl-friends. And that was the hardest, no girlfriends.

What Were The Three Easiest Things About Marine Basic?

On an overcast day when everything was gray, and cold
I have seen a blazing cross a pink light on the horizon
everything coated with ice. This happened on Thanks-
giving and it made it easy to believe in Jesus.

                                                       Church
was one of the easiest things in Marine Basic. You sat
in a soft chair in an auditorium listening to a minister's
voice come to put you to sleep, and you would be in a
small town in Illinois on a lazy summer day.

                                                     Sleeping. It
was absolutely the easiest thing to do. You became so tired
you could sleep standing up, sleep marching. You could sleep
on firewatch duty. When your head hit the pillow in fifteen
minutes you were in dream land dreaming about food.

                                                        Eating.
Eating Thanksgiving dinner. All that delectable mouthwatering
food. Eating was always easy because I got extra potatoes, bread
and cake. The tables were spread with a Thanksgiving day feast
and we thanked Jesus, ate heartily and then rested.

The Fighter Pilot

This fighter jet
curves in space
in front of you
a green camouflage.
Roaring like a lion
soaring through august clouds.
He might be a fighter pilot.
A one star General
waking up in the hospital
bed beside you.
He might laugh
and tell you
he likes to wear his hair short
because it is cool under his helmet,
his white pilot helmet.
The fighter pilot
might be recovering
from kidney surgery
on the same day as you.
This might be real
or it might be a dream.

Two Creeds

Drill Instructor's Creed:
These are my recruits.
I will train them
to the best of my ability.
I will develop them into
smartly disciplined,
physically fit, basically
trained Marines, thoroughly
indoctrinated in love
of God, country and corps.
I will demand of them and
demonstrate by my own example,
the highest standards of
personal conduct, morality
and professional skill.

The Recruit's Creed:
To be a Marine
you have to believe in
yourself, your fellow Marine
your corps, your country, your God,
semper fidelis.

Graduation

In the night sky Cassiopeia, Cygnus, Draco and the Big
Dipper visible. Last night we saw those together; looking
at constellations like connect the dots. Graduation is
the brightest sun shining, gooseflesh jubilant, shouting
for joy day in my life. In the morning we showered, put
on our best dress uniform and prepared to march together
that one last time to our rite of passage ceremony. Our
faces beaming hope, our creases sharp, when Gunnery Ser-
geant Sentinella called, "PLA — TOON 3183, FALL — IN."
Marching at the front of the platoon was Private First
Class Kennedy wearing the Honor Blues, carrying a guidon
with our flag marching beside Gunny Sentinella who carried
his Marine sword. Four platoons were graduating and in
silence we listened for our C.O. at long last to say,
"Congratulations Marines."

We shouted, jumped up and down, and tossed our covers
into the leatherneck, jarhead, devildog, sky. Then, one-
by-one shook hands with our DI whose olive green stripes
were crossing on the field of red.

Where
The River Flows

for Spirit and February

3039-PEAR

spring

snowbank

a long yellow line of
cactus flowers
it is sad the beatles
can not get back
electric solar cars
come on come on
snare drums high hats
with soft brushes
crack the sky for j.l.
needles rise above
pine cones frozen in
ice a ray of light
a million voices

the hump on his back

around the corner
like winter
the first day of spring
disappears

a man limps by
with a wooden cane
his snowwhite hair
does not touch

a tropical shower

banana plants bell shaped
fleshy fruit are edible raw
more than two happy monkeys
could consume in moonlight
under green skin

a complacent lion
distills a shadow of delightful
giraffes sensing danger
in their camouflage
the river runs cold

when a family
of ivory tusked elephants
spray themselves with water
and trumpet
four blue zebras sprint away

malvinas

it was some great dysfunction.
what would *you* do,
bored out of your mind
with infinity
by distracted disciplines of
recalcitrant winds?

an odd radiance
from these accidental outcrops
debris from *continental drift.*

bamboo art

the problem with it is
there's no way of telling
exactly where the water
begins or where it ends
the fish are swimming
along and suddenly
out of nowhere comes
this flower this rose
and another and another
and the third
has no color that is
to say it's the same
as the water

one year of grace

try to imagine
one year of grace
one perfect day after another

in a house where dust
does not collect behind walls
and the corners are free from webs

when you enter here take off your shoes
the floors are made of gold
hidden in the carpenter's truth

for we are gifted
with felicity of
place of solitude

& friends
and what we store
in memory

and I think
with patience
and with kindness
what is possible becomes new

colorado university

my daughter taps the ship's bell
which is low within her reach
as we enter the glenn miller lounge
at the university memorial center
we glance at his trombone and some
fading photographs of his childhood
glenn and helen are golden buff graduates
it is one happily married couple's
achievement to be immortalized
we put a coin in the juke box
like an echo trapped in a canyon
the air if full of swing

where the river flows

the heady water lilies
know this old river
carries silt
to an island that drifts
downstream

and spring floods will rise
under a bridge
and grind boulders

and they know meadows
and children who dance in a circle

hiking to cahokia

I went with scout troop 103
to cahokia
huge mounds date back
to precolumbian time
our leader an ex-marine sergeant
kept us going over rough terrain
25 miles from the mounds
marching is meant to develop character
to make good citizens

spring on the illinois prairie
a mist drifting overhead
the sun burned it away
by late morning we tramped
then what seemed
footprints of vanished races
an endless trail
along an unbroken canal bank

we ate at the excavations
then began digging around for arrowheads
who knows where this nation vanished to
what vision their people had
or what their language was
all I know is
who ever they were
their dead are buried
in these pyramids

snapshot

my mom's photo
me with curly blond hair
a smiling face
a crimson telephone

improvisation on birthmarks & body scars

a razor cut nighthawk
glides uplifting currents
on my thumb
    the birthmark on my spine
    is the continent out back
a scar on my finger is
the shape of a dueling pistol
    the scalpel slice on my left abdomen
    is a surgeon's
    his hands
    slipped into my side
    and lifted out my kidney
    bringing it to me in a bottle
the birthmark on my right upper thigh
peeks out when I wear shorts
it is a question mark
mutating into a pyramid
a mysterious eye staring from the point

sweet trees fragrant trees

in spring a cigar tree
drops popcorn petals
near my home
peach pear sycamore
boxelder mulberry cherry
and plum bloom
in the neighborhood
of home

summer

western light

yet becoming aware
of the magnetic
western light's musk sundown
horizontal spread

they watch a western scene
from "lodestone"
and share a box
of hot buttered corn

next door the fiftynine chevy
bel-air windows steam
and the seats squeak
another horizontal spread
of hot buttered corn

and speaking loud
the western impulse vibrates
a woman wiping away tears waves
to the cowboy riding into the sunset

hand poems

slender fingertips
grasp dust and ashes
rub a blind eyelid
touch a deaf ear
gnarled veins
distorted knuckles
the carpenter works outdoors
on sawhorses or at supper
holds an avocado

the 4th of july

at carnival
a clown
said of a sad clown
he thinks he is
and all the clowns
gathered in a clump
to blow their balloons up
and twist them
into shapes of animals
when a fifteen foot
uncle sam on stilts
spread his legs
to let spiderman through
my daughter wondered
how he got out of our tv

at the fireworks display
everyone said ou and ah

dream of chicago

john who did not die in the afternoon
tim who wrote the first buzzard novel
went to chicago to visit the pope
there was joy in mass and
shoulder to shoulder people sang
with john paul II
he sang a polish folk tune

the pope gave his blessing
and everyone left in secret

now children are happy and sing
the clouds are full of rain

earth

the four winds blow
in harmony
a gentle river
a cottonwood too

before the strike

summer without ball
it must be heavenly
why my friend bob
phones offering box
seats at wrigley
field lou brock
signs my daughter's program
rain comes off the lake
in the 5th inning
we go home wet

prescription for nuclear attack

if you are driving
stop your car
on interstate 57
take off your cubs tee shirt
dip the shirt in
wrap it wet around your face
if you are still alive
search for survivors

interviewing an air force
hospital handy man

he speaks about v.j. day
on the streets of honolulu
without batting an eye
wears oshkosh denims to work
has his own tool shop
logs onehundred & fifty thousand miles
in his checker car
earl is a handy man

who says most poetry bores him
and people should follow the ten commandments

as he repairs the heel of a nurse's shoe

the lyricist

a bluecollar worker said
I can't get a good shave
with this razor
what I need is a straight edge
packing his bag he left
in new jersey he became a songwriter
using a cherrywood piano
lonely he walked an elegant dalmation
lit his pipe
studied the stars
wrote songs
and fed sparky

letter to rich

you send an address
I don't answer your letter
the girls are happy
labor day we went to
bloomington where the lions
and elks live in a zoo
I've been hoeing weeds
watching the cumulus ascend
thinking about the future

under northern lights

from kansas after sundown
riderless horses
graze the short prairie grass
under northern lights
men dressed in royal blue they
sleep sitting as if in haste
a breeze bends the grasstops
miles across the plains across
the missouri where sioux nations camp
smoke rolls out of a wigwam
sunlight darkens the
turquoise sky
the cavalry climb on their saddles
and ride toward st. louis

8

how is it we can
see the rough spots
when we look back

I'm here dad
I am here
I'm glad you are here

concord is silent now
mt. st. helens is too
and does not rasp a warning

pressures melt basalt
floating ash creates
a brilliant sunset
a cool summer dusk

red and you stop
green and you go
dad the clouds are harmless
green and you go

crimson

I would touch you
the way that sunshine
touches grass
the grass holds
a shield of dew
that prisms light into crystal
or I would touch you
as shade from an olive
tree that cools two lions

or I would touch you
the way two dolphins
touch water
as they swim in and out
of the water in circles
around a pool

or the way two cardinals
one the female gray and red
one the male bright red
touch their young
I would see you
with my words

cavefish for l.l.

seeing nothing
the cavefish
in deep ocean caves
unaware of your poems
sleep with their eyes open

solar complexities

you skindive
in coastal coral waters

I emerge
in cultures and other circles

neptune slowly evolves
continents change their shape

religious cults
seek islands for suicide

starfish hang
on piers where smoked fish are sold

glaciers float
in atlantic currents

you sit on a bench
in a midwestern park

I search the night sky
where stars are pebbles

fall

the maxillofacial surgeon's dog

I cry
like a young raven
as elevator doors open
medics
dressed in white
wheel a gory body

something about love
says you cannot lock me

conversations float
across tables

the surgeon says
I sewed her face up
talks of his
big
dog

who waits
on the front porch
saying haha
I climbed the fence

I say
love
as sweet pears
cling full ripe
to their tree

rain clouds

rain
clouds are in a jagged sky
corn stalks are dry
up to their golden ears
above they are green
mighty strange around here
less than a trace this month

hard corn

o they are sleek
taking summer trips to
paducah the sun capitol
of illinois
the government gives surplus grain
to sell for crops they didn't plant
like pharaoh's granaries
these yellow trucks with silver dish hubs
arrive in caravans of dieseling chrome stacks
to haul the grain to heaven

o but they have their troubles too
when the mud is deep at calving time
and mothers lose their calves' scent
and won't let them suck
they die by thousands
and at harvest time
when the orange moon pulls its shoulder
& powerful trucks fall
& rip apart hard
corn spews over all creation

chicken soup

in indian summer
start with one carrot
in a big pot add
one onion two potatoes
a large chicken breast
a few greenbeans
listen to a piano sonata
a trombone a clarinet
add three cups of water
one handful of rice
three ripe tomatoes
salt and pepper to taste
simmer all evening
go out to the porch
have a glass of cider
breathe deep the autumn air
and feel the chill

hallowed wood

the wind scatters
a candleflame frown

I listen for the cry of
a hungry screech owl

stalking field mice
among the timber shadows

to hint of deep winter

de de who is almost four
found a single violet
it was an autumn stem
she would not pick

she says we are
two hungry hippos

petting a bulldog
she says he had curly hair
and laughs

american gothic

farmer brown
is holding his
fork and mother
is looking
away
she's in soybean
heaven
where the hay
stack is
I'd paint a
huge stack
of salvador dali heads
and two giraffes' heads
on fire in the loft
using the artist's
parents
as models

pyromaniac

a holocaust of institution's
destructive power

why couldn't the detectives
figure it out
he always flees the scene
on his honda
then returns to carry hoses
from the hook and ladder truck
a million in damages
and his picture
on the front page

the fragrant bouquet of
gasoline splashes
the igneous magnitude
blue flame
blazes from room to room
he wants to walk out
barefoot
on coals white hot
to go through fire

liberty

picture a van gogh scene
the paris café at night
a french sculptor
sits at table talking about his sculpture
the lovely lady of liberty

it was my gift to america
it stands now at bedloe's island
a torch upraised
a book in the other arm
you see her when you come into the harbor

my friend toulouse
went wild over her
she's a symbol
an electrical conductor
made of copper

a basic element
one capacitor
looking over the city
reaching up to the skyline
like a huge lightning rod

a few pennies
and a five dollar bill

comes this man
with a few pennies
a five dollar bill in his pocket
who is not surprised
when pigs & chickens wander the street
and he rents a law office
on the corner of 6th street
finds himself a statesman senior who
before departing to washingon
spends his last night in springfield
in the lindsay home
thinking if only I lived in another era
but this was war & the lines on his face
dream mud streets
around small country cabins
where happiness
is a pig and three chickens

nightsound

while my children sleep
alex laughs on the phone
he is a gentle man
after we hang up
there is a silence
a night breeze
a curtain moves
crickets begin to sing
across the field
a truck's amber lights
disappear under a bridge
a distant muffle
my shoes are wet with dew
I look up at the stars
and the new position
of the planets

timbre

the timbre
of two part harmony
makes me smile

all the way home
those years ago

and now the voices
they sing
and Jesus is talking to his dad
somewhere a cloud floats
up in sunlight

my old friend comes back again
and she
has large curls
they fall around her shoulders

and memories of wicker chairs

along our journey
into blue mountains

digging up wildcherry wine

instead of stealing pumpkins
or soaping windows
we meet on halloween
to dig up the wildcherry wine
that patrick david and I
buried in a five gallon
crock jar
on a sweltering humid day

dry oak leaves
rattle as limbs crack
in a chilly autumn breeze
we dig on the spot
where the ground is swollen

staked out in a stubble cornfield
a lonely scarecrow
wears a farmer's bib overalls
he protects us from
wolves bats and green mist

winter

in this greenhouse

a skeleton frame
was made of weathered boards
and glass saved from
abandoned store front windows
where seasons don't intrude
neighboring farmers
come and smoke their pipes
among the greenpeppers

in winter
the window people
come here to eat potatoes
and zucchini squashbread
they read poems aloud
to the plants

iron toe

the ute in
the mountain wears
a blue
            and white striped
                blanket

his arms folded
            over his stomach
                toes up

dreaming
pulled wedge weave

he sleeps
            with braids on a
                boulder

in the fieldhouse

she is stretching
in her martial arts tunic

why do I notice
dirt on the sole of her foot

and the cobalt depth
of those eyes

she asks me
if I am training for a marathon

gives me daylight
between wind sprints

november

we munch molasses cookies
shapes of oak leaves
and the horn of plenty
we sip cranberry tea
not seeing each other
in eight years we have nothing
to say ask me what is
my favorite jogging shoe
I walk you to your car
the ground is covered with snow
we hug and I wonder
why have you come back
on the roof of your car
is a yellow canoe
a gift from your parents
to your husband

a covered bridge in winter

blue snow blue starry sky

the covered bridge is empty
as we approach electric candles
light the white houses closeby

the whole covered bridge
is alight with christmas decorations
the bridge glows softly in the blue snow

we pass through the bridge together

3039-PEAR

nichols park

for steve lowe

our plan was to meet here
when the war was over
I return in the heart of winter
skater's blades scar the pond's surface
and the ferris wheel remains
as one unmovable gawk
in summer we rode that ferris wheel
with our dates
into the night's fireworks
the wheel's neon lights spinning
like tracers in the dark
in this grim winter
the only visual is a name
eli bridge company
riveted to a crossbar
before entering the pavilion
I stop for a moment
at the tree that was planted for you
when I go inside
a cracked ball mirror spins
on the ceiling
throws violet light on me

a cultural sponge

london bridge came
shipped stone by stone
to arizona
in an american winter
whose idea was this
ya'll in sun city
visit the bridge
spanning the desert
imagine the palace guard marching
the queen is having tea
I stand aside cheering
the british start a revolution
a movement
to recover the colonies

sleigh ride in illinois

on the hill with a new blue
sled in the fresh snow
a child listens to the roar
of the winds ripping through
tree limbs bringing out the blush
on her cheeks she pushes off
downhill on a short silent ride

goods & services

ok so much for
local merchants town squares
cracker barrels & a
chaw of tobacco
now they tell me that
our televisions are to be
connected to a central computer
if we need groceries
we push a button
money will be transferred
by microchip
likewise our groceries
I'm not against it
but we may get some bad fruit
and our clothes may not fit
and perhaps
computer crime will rise
as for community well
we'll have more time
to watch the NFL
to tune in
"auction for the arts"
and to hush our kids so
we can listen

the view from my window

last night
a spring thaw came
along the western landscape
a crow landed in a bare maple
then flew over a field
the light gleams
on wet pavement
on parking lot lines
on the back of a stop sign
underground
the tulips are growing